Build It So They Can Play

Affordable Equipment for Adapted Physical Education

Teresa Sullivan

Cindy Slagle

T.J. Hapshie

Debbie Brevard

Vic Brevard

Human Kinetics

Library of Congress Cataloging-in-Publication Data

Build it so they can play : affordable equipment for adapted physical education / Teresa Sullivan
. . . [et al.].

   p. cm.
  ISBN-13: 978-0-7360-8991-3 (soft cover)
  ISBN-10: 0-7360-8991-8 (soft cover)
  1. Physical education for children with disabilities. 2. Physical education and training--
Equipment and supplies. 3. Sporting goods. 4. Motor learning. I. Sullivan, Teresa, 1972-
GV445.B78 2012
  371.904486--dc23

2011034865

ISBN-10: 0-7360-8991-8 (print)
ISBN-13: 978-0-7360-8991-3 (print)

The web addresses cited in this text were current as of October 2011, unless otherwise noted.

Acquisitions Editor: Cheri Scott; **Developmental Editor:** Jacqueline Eaton Blakley; **Assistant Editor:** Anne Rumery; **Copyeditor:** Jan Feeney; **Permissions Manager:** Dalene Reeder; **Graphic Designer:** Fred Starbird; **Graphic Artist:** Kathleen Boudreau-Fuoss, **Cover Designer:** Keith Blomberg; **Photographers (cover):** Kristen Cottrell and Teresa Sullivan; **Photographers (interior):** Teresa Sullivan, Cindy Slagle, T.J. Hapshie, Debbie Brevard, and Vic Brevard; **Art Manager:** Kelly Hendren; **Associate Art Manager:** Alan L. Wilborn; **Illustrations:** © Human Kinetics; **Printer:** United Graphics

Printed in the United States of America   10 9 8 7 6 5 4 3 2 1

The paper in this book is certified under a sustainable forestry program.

Human Kinetics
Website: www.HumanKinetics.com

United States: Human Kinetics
P.O. Box 5076
Champaign, IL 61825-5076
800-747-4457
e-mail: humank@hkusa.com

Canada: Human Kinetics
475 Devonshire Road Unit 100
Windsor, ON N8Y 2L5
800-465-7301 (in Canada only)
e-mail: info@hkcanada.com

Europe: Human Kinetics
107 Bradford Road
Stanningley
Leeds LS28 6AT, United Kingdom
+44 (0) 113 255 5665
e-mail: hk@hkeurope.com

Australia: Human Kinetics
57A Price Avenue
Lower Mitcham, South Australia 5062
08 8372 0999
e-mail: info@hkaustralia.com

New Zealand: Human Kinetics
P.O. Box 80
Torrens Park, South Australia 5062
0800 222 062
e-mail: info@hknewzealand.com

E5036

Contents

chapter 1

Equipment for Sport and Recreation Activities 1

chapter 2

Modified Equipment for Sport and Recreation Activities 43

chapter 3

Modified Equipment for Vestibular and Fine Motor Activities 65

chapter 4

Sensory Equipment 95

Equipment Finder

All equipment can be used in a general physical education classroom. Some equipment is designed or modified for individuals with specific disabilities so they can participate in a general physical education class.

Disability or Condition

AMP amputations

VI visual impairment

CB congenital birth defects

AU autism

CP cerebral palsy

LCF limited cognitive functioning

LRM limited range of motion

NA nonambulatory

G general or all-purpose (no disability or condition)

CP cerebral palsy

Need

CC cardio condition

Ba balance

EH eye-hand coordination

Fx flexibility

EF eye-foot coordination

GF general fitness

MP motor planning

VS visual stimulation

TS tactile stimulation

AS auditory stimulation

Equipment	Disability	Need	Page
Action and reaction board	General	EH, VS, TS	90
Ambulatory trainer	VI, CP, NA	Ba, EF, MP	108
Balance beams	General	EH, MP, Ba	84
Balance boards	General	Ba, EF	80
Balance stools	General	Ba, EF, MP, TS	82
Ball drop	AMP, CP, LCF, LRM, NA	EH, MP, VS, TS	52
Big foot	General	Ba, EF, MP	70
Bombs away	General	EH, VS, MP	34
Box hockey	General	EH, MP	10
Box top hockey	General	EH, MP	4
Combination lock trainer	General	EH, MP	66
Cooperative walking boards	General	Ba, EF, MP, TS	72
Duct tape juggling	General	EH, MP	54
Fishing	General	EH, MP	27
Flat straps	General	EH, VS, TS	97
Four up and four down	General	EH, Fx, MP	36

Equipment	Disability	Need	Page
Giant beads	General	EH, VS, TS	86
Giant ring slide stand	General	EH, MP, TS	88
Hockey stick and puck	General, AMP, CB, NA, LRM	EH, MP	62
Hole-in-one target ball	AU, CP, NA	EH, MP, EF	19
Hook 'n' lasso golf	General	EH, MP	20
Hose rocket (zip-line)	VI, CP, LRM	CC, Fx, MP	26
Hula hoop basketball	AMP, VI, CP, NA, LRM	EH, MP	48
Hula hoop mobile	VI, CB, LCF, NA	EH, Fx, MP, VS, TS	98
Modified jump ropes	AMP, CP, LRM, VI, AU, LCF	CC, EH, EF, Ba, GF	56
Modified pull-up bar	VI, CB, LRM	GF	50
Modified wristband	VI, LCF	VS, AS	105
Moon rocks	AU	Ba, EF, MP	79
Monster truck	AMP, VI, CB, CP	Ba, VS, AS	60
Movable basketball goal	General	EH	6
Movable ring toss	General	CC, EH, MP	32
Peg boards	VI, AU	EH	87
Plunger horseshoes	General	EH	5
Portable A-frame stand	General	EH, MP	102
PVC bowling ramp	LRM, LCF, NA, AMP, VI, AU, CB, CP	MP	44
Rainmaker and sensory bottle	LRM, NA, LCF	VS, TS	114
Recycled beanbag toss	General	EH, MP	22
Ring toss	General	EH, MP	30
Scooter chair	AMP, VI, CB, CP	CC, Ba	64
Sensory balls	VI, LCF, LRM	VS, TS	117
Sensory box	VI, LCF, LRM, NA, AU, general	EH, MP, TS, VS	116
Sensory lap towel	VI, LCF, LRM	VS, TS	119
Sensory lap tray	VI, LCF, LRM	VS, TS	118
Sensory room	VI, LCF, LRM	VS, TS	106
Shuffleboard stick	General	EH, MP	53
Six-sided hockey	General	EH	12
Soccer goals	General	CC, EF, GF	14
Stepping stones	General	Ba, GF, MP	78
Table racing	AMP, CB, NA, LRM, General	CC, MP	28
Tabletop basketball goal	CB, General, NA	EH, MP	8

(continued)

Equipment	Disability	Need	Page
Tactile mat	VI, CB, LCF, NA	TS, VS	112
Therapy bed	NA	Fx, VS, TS	110
Tinikling bars	General	EF, CC, MP, GF	15
Trash can basketball backboard	AMP, NA, LRM	EH, GF	2
Tug-a-play	VI, LRM	EH, GF, MP	68
Under an umbrella	VI, LCF, LRM	VS, TS	100
Up-and-down board	AU, LCF, general	Ba, EH, MP, EF	74
Vestibular board	General	Ba	69
Vic's tennis ball foosball	General	EH, MP, GF	16
Washtub fun	LCF, general	Ba, EF	76
Washers	General	EH, MP	24
Wonderland board game	LRM, LCF, NA, AMP, VI, AU, CB, CP	NP	40
Wooden bowling ramp	General	EH, MP	46

Foreword

Lauren J. Lieberman, PhD

For many years I have taught children with severe and multiple disabilities in both inclusive and segregated settings. Thinking of ways to integrate these children into the curriculum in any placement of physical education has been a struggle for teachers for years.

The authors—Teresa Sullivan, Cindy Slagle, T.J. Hapshie, Vic Brevard, and Debbie Brevard—are teachers who came together and created an avenue for including, inspiring, and challenging children with and without disabilities. The creativity, imagination, and commitment that these teachers have shown over the years are unequaled.

I first saw a presentation by this team at the Texas Alliance for Health, Physical Education, Recreation and Dance conference. They put together everyday items so that children could jump rope, throw, bounce, do strength activities, engage in cognitive tasks, and tackle everyday units, and it was remarkable. Sullivan and company have amazing ideas for both fine motor and gross motor activities as well as balance and sensory skills for all children. I shared my enthusiasm with the staff at our New York State headquarters; shortly thereafter we invited the team to the New York State AHPERD conference, where attendees had the opportunity to make and use PVC bowling ramps, step catchers, and sensory PVC hangers. The attendees frantically wrote down instructions. I told this team that they *had* to write a book. These activities and modifications were so creative and inexpensive that teachers needed to learn about them.

The next year, at the AAHPERD conference, Sullivan and her colleagues' presentation was packed with eager teachers. The authors have worked hard to get their amazing ideas on paper so they could share their joy, imagination, equipment, and creative activities with other teachers.

You will be awed by how everyday items can be cut, tied, glued, or bent so that children with even the most severe disabilities can do things they never did before. If a child can't get a ball into a 10-foot basket, you will learn how to put the basket on a scooter and bring it to the child. If a child can't jump over a rope, you will learn how to cut the rope in half so he doesn't have to jump. If a child has a visual impairment and can't see the rope, you'll know how to add a quarter of a hula hoop to the rope so it doesn't get tangled and so the child can hear the rope hit the floor for rhythm.

This amazing team of authors shows how to make goals, horseshoes, sticks, catapults, throwing implements, recreational backyard games, and more with little or no money. Now children with even severe disabilities can play soccer, hockey, basketball, and many recreational games. The instructions are easy to follow. You also have access to modifications to the games so that you can accommodate a variety of disabilities.

Whether you are a teacher, parent, teacher's aide, therapist, or professional preparation student, this book will open up your mind and excite your imagination. With a little time, energy, and innovation, all of your students will be active participants in any game or activity in your curriculum.

Preface

Educators often face difficulties in securing the resources they need in order to teach effectively. This is especially true of physical educators, who rely on equipment to help young people develop and practice physical skills. And it's all the more so in adapted physical education, where modified and specialized equipment can be costly but is essential in order for educators to serve the developmental needs (and IEP goals) of students with disabilities. Unfortunately, the cost of physical education equipment continues to rise as funding continues to be reduced or even eliminated, and modified equipment costs even more than general equipment. What's a teacher to do?

Build It So They Can Play is a collaboration of ideas for building affordable equipment that can be used by teachers and individuals working with students with disabilities, whether in physical education, adapted physical education, or community recreation. Using inexpensive supplies such as PVC pipes and plywood, for example, you can construct physical education equipment that is easily adapted to students' individual needs. Everyday objects—even things that would otherwise be thrown away—can be repurposed and made useful. A trash can becomes a mobile low basketball goal with a piece of plywood and a screwdriver. An umbrella is transformed into a sensory mobile with nothing more than some zip ties and objects of varying textures. You can even save money by constructing your own therapy bed that gives students who use wheelchairs the opportunity to get out of the chair without lying on the floor. This book is full of ideas for enhancing your collection of adapted physical education supplies in a way that fits into any budget!

All equipment described in this book has proved successful in physical education environments. In addition, the equipment is easily modified and individualized so that all students can experience success in any environment. Most of the equipment is easy to make, while some pieces require a bit more complex assembly. Diagrams and photos are included to give you a visual guide. And each description features ideas for using the equipment and customizing it for various abilities and purposes.

Chapter 1 focuses on building equipment that can be used for specific sport and recreation activities. Chapter 2 shows ways to modify or build equipment to be used in general sport and recreation activities. In chapter 3 you will find equipment to aid with vestibular and fine motor development. Chapter 4 covers equipment that can be used with sensory activities that foster audio-visual and tactile stimulation. An appendix offers creative ideas for repurposing common, inexpensive, or free objects for use in physical education activities, and an equipment finder guides you in finding the equipment and activities that suit your students' particular needs.

Everyone can create a better way of teaching. All it takes is creativity! Any student can be successful doing physical activities. Place yourself in the students' shoes. Assumptions must be challenged in order for progress to occur. Limitations are road blocks, and as a teacher you must discover a way to accomplish your goal: providing a positive physical education experience to all students regardless of limitations or disabilities.

Acknowledgments

The authors would like to acknowledge and thank their families, friends, and fellow teachers for their encouragement and support.

A special thanks to Dr. Lauren Lieberman, who encouraged us to write this book. You are an inspiration. We admire and respect you for all you do to promote the field of adapted physical education.

Equipment for Sport and Recreation Activities

This chapter offers instructions on creating equipment to use in playing certain sport and recreation activities. Equipment is cost effective, easy to make, and portable enough to be used in any learning environment. The following pages give you the tools for creating equipment that will inspire students to participate in the activities.

Trash Can
Basketball Backboard

NEED AND DISABILITY

Trash can basketball is a great activity for students in wheelchairs and is fun for students of all ability levels. Students have the opportunity to develop eye–hand coordination and teamwork while experiencing success. It's also a great lead-up game for learning basketball.

TOOLS

Circular saw or hand saw, tape measure, Phillips screwdriver

SUPPLIES

Floor tape (any color)

1 piece of 1/4-inch plywood or paneling 3 by 3 feet

1 piece of 4-1/4-inch round molding

6 1/2-inch Phillips head wood screws or wood glue

1 32-gallon trash can (or whatever size you have available)

INSTRUCTIONS

1. Cut 1/4-inch plywood or paneling to the size and shape of a basketball backboard approximately 2 feet high and 3 feet long.
2. Cut two 1-by-6-inch slits or grooves about 12 inches apart on bottom of backboard, as shown in the diagram.
3. Glue or screw the 1/4-inch molding to back of board just above slits. The molding stabilizes the backboard on the trash can. If using screws, be sure to put them in from the front of the backboard so that they are flush and won't interfere with play.
4. Mark a rectangle approximately 12 inches wide by 9 inches tall on the backboard for students to use as a target when shooting.
5. Mount backboard on trash can using the slits on the backboard.

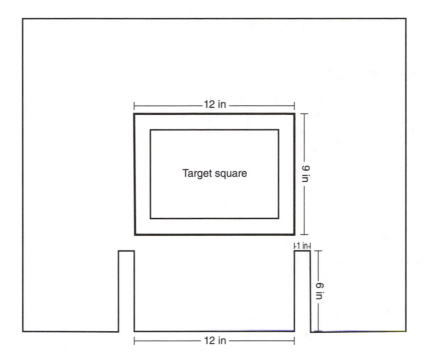

▶ IDEAS FOR USING THIS EQUIPMENT

- Play basketball using the regulation rules.
- Play HORSE or around the world.

▶ MODIFICATIONS

If you have limited space, you can modify the size of the backboard and trash can.

Box Top Hockey

▶NEED AND DISABILITY

This game involves students of all abilities. This game can be played on any area and on any surface. Students with emerging skills will work on eye–hand coordination and sportsmanship.

▶TOOLS

None needed

▶SUPPLIES

   1 box lid (such as from a computer paper box; a variety of sizes will work)

   1 marker

   1 plastic bottle cap

▶INSTRUCTIONS

   1. Turn box lid upside down.

   2. Draw the floor layout of hockey rink. You can make it as detailed as you would like (halfcourt lines, penalty lines, and so on).

   3. Use the upside-down bottle cap as a puck.

▶IDEAS FOR USING THIS EQUIPMENT

Place box on table. Two partners take turns thumping cap with fingers. Strikers (such as jar lids) could be used to score goals in goal lines.

Plunger Horseshoes

▶ NEED AND DISABILITY

This is a tool for students of all abilities. Students with emerging skills have the opportunity to work on balance and coordination. This is an inexpensive way to generate active participation in the general physical education setting.

▶ TOOLS

None needed

▶ SUPPLIES

2 plungers

6 plastic horseshoes or deck rings

▶ INSTRUCTIONS

1. Place plungers as far apart as appropriate for ability of students.
2. Plungers should be suctioned to stick to floor.
3. Plungers will stand on carpeted floors.
4. Students throw horseshoes toward plungers, just as in a regular game of horseshoes.

▶ IDEAS FOR USING THIS EQUIPMENT

Use rules for indoor horseshoes. The winning team is the one who hooks the most rings over the plungers.

▶ MODIFICATIONS

Use circle rings or swim flotation rings or swim diving rings instead of horseshoes.

Movable Basketball Goal

▶NEED AND DISABILITY

This is for students of all abilities. Students with emerging skills have the opportunity to work on eye–hand coordination, teamwork, and ball skills.

▶TOOLS

Hand saw or PVC pipe cutter, screwdriver, tape measure

▶SUPPLIES

1 scooter board 12 by 12 inches

1 1/2-inch dowel rod 6 inches long

1 1-inch PVC pipe 10 feet long

3 1-inch T-joints

8 1-inch 90-degree elbow joints

1 small net or plastic bag

3 or 4 small screws or PVC glue

6 to 8 zip ties

▶INSTRUCTIONS

1. Cut 1-inch PVC into one 4-foot length, two 8-inch lengths, eight 4-inch lengths, and two 3-inch lengths. Attach as shown in the photo.

2. Drill 1/2-inch hole in bottom of 4-foot section of PVC. Push 4-foot section into predrilled hole of scooter board. Push dowel rod through hole to keep PVC from falling down through hole of scooter board.

3. Hang net or plastic bag from one or both goals, used to catch balls, and attach with zip ties if needed. Gluing the top portion of the goals will make traveling easier.

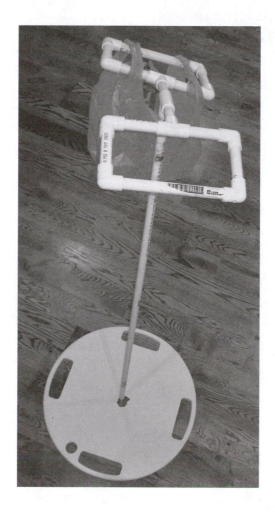

▶ IDEAS FOR USING THIS EQUIPMENT

- While standing on spots, students use the basket as a target as it moves past them.
- Play scooter basketball while someone else controls the rolling basketball goal.

▶ MODIFICATIONS

Anchor goal so it will not move. When you use it with students with lower ability, a goal that is not moving makes it easier for students to be successful.

Tabletop Basketball Goal

▶ NEED AND DISABILITY

Tabletop basketball is a portable game that can be played on a wheelchair tray or table surface. It's ideal for students who have limited hand motion. Once the ball on the spoon is aimed at the backboard or basket, all that is required is the flick of a finger. The game helps students develop eye–hand coordination and sportsmanship.

▶ TOOLS

Hand or electric saw, screwdriver, electric drill and bit, tape measure, hammer

▶ SUPPLIES

1 piece of pine wood 2 by 4 by 10 inches (base of game)

1 piece of MDF board 3/8 by 4 by 4 inches (backboard)

1 ½-inch dowel rod 11 inches long (goalpost)

1 2-inch PVC pipe 3/8 inch long (sliver) (basketball goal)

1 1-inch wooden ball (basketball)

1 piece of string 15 inches long

1 plastic spoon

1 tube of wood glue

1 small nail (the size used to hang a picture frame)

1 #4 ½-inch screw

▶ INSTRUCTIONS

1. Drill 1/2-inch hole in 2-by-4 at one end to support goalpost. Cut a slit at a 45-degree angle to house spoon on opposite end from goal.

2. Cut MDF into basketball backboard shape approximately 4 by 4 inches and rounded on top.

3. Attach backboard to dowel rod (goalpost) with glue and nail.

4. Attach 2-inch PVC (goal rim) to backboard using 1/2-inch screw.

5. Insert goalpost into hole in 2-by-4.

6. Drill a small hole in wooden ball. Glue the string to the inside of the hole. With glue and nail, attach the other end of the string under goal at goalpost.

7. Insert flat end of spoon in slit of 2-by-4.

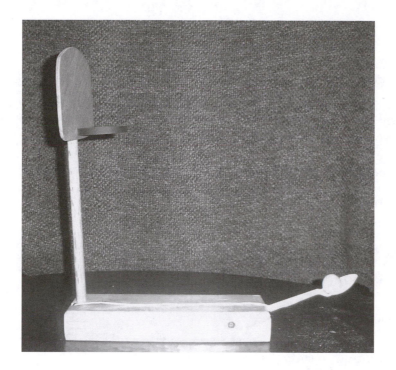

▶ IDEAS FOR USING THIS EQUIPMENT

Play a mini-basketball game. Use tally scoring to set a game-winning number.

Box Hockey

NEED AND DISABILITY

This is a game for students with and without intellectual disabilities. Game strategies and competition come into play with the higher-level students. In students of lower skill levels, eye–hand coordination and upper-body strength are developed. For those of any skill level, the game combines teamwork with friendly competition.

TOOLS

Hand saw or electric saw, hammer, tape measure

SUPPLIES

3 boards 1 inch by 6 inches by 8 feet

Box of 2-inch nails

2 1-inch dowel rods

1 nut (used as a puck—choose whatever size works best for your students, or get nuts in several sizes)

INSTRUCTIONS

1. Cut boards into two 4-foot lengths and four 3-foot lengths.
2. Cut half circle for goals on two of the 3-foot-long boards. You can use a 1-gallon paint can or coffee can as a template. Assemble as shown in the diagram.
3. Cut half circles in the two remaining 3-foot boards as shown in the diagram.
4. Hammer nails from the outside of frame to the two 4-foot-long boards aligning the 3-foot-long boards. Players can use dowel rods to hit the nut.

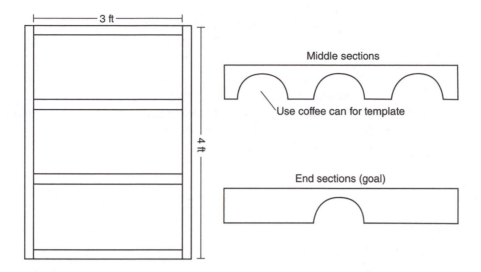

IDEAS FOR USING THIS EQUIPMENT

Position one student on each side of box hockey frame with a dowel rod. Place the nut in the middle. Students hit the nut at the same time, trying to score a goal in end goals.

MODIFICATIONS

Rather than a nut, use a slightly bigger object that might roll to assist with movement around the board (e.g., soda bottle cap, miniature plastic hockey puck).

Six-Sided Hockey

▶NEED AND DISABILITY

This is a game for students of all abilities. Students with emerging skills will work on color identification, eye–hand coordination, accuracy, and teamwork. Students in wheelchairs could be out of their chairs on the floor to participate with their peers who are not in wheelchairs.

▶TOOLS

Hand saw or electric saw, screwdriver, tape measure, paint supplies

▶SUPPLIES

6 boards 1 inch by 6 inches by 5 feet

6 3-inch hinges

6 different colors of indoor or outdoor latex paint

30 varieties of balls colored to match goals in the game (such as foam, Softi balls, Wiffle balls)

▶INSTRUCTIONS

1. The 1-inch-by-6-inch-by-5-foot boards can be purchased in this size. If not, cut boards to 5-foot lengths.

2. Cut out half circles for goals. A coffee can is a good template for the half circle.

3. Paint each board a different color.

4. Attach two boards together at the ends of the boards with one of the hinges. Repeat this step with the remaining two pairs of boards. Each of these joints will be permanent.

5. Take the three remaining hinges and remove pins. Attach hinges without pins to ends of boards. Pins can be put back in as assembly of game is needed. Making every other connection removable allows for easy travel.

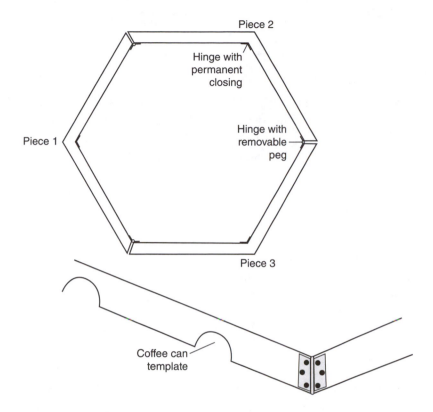

Piece 2

Hinge with permanent closing

Hinge with removable peg

Piece 1

Piece 3

Coffee can template

▶ IDEAS FOR USING THIS EQUIPMENT

With two to twelve players, use your hand or short hockey sticks (hand size) to knock balls out of the circle through the openings before your opponent does. Defend the goals while at same time pushing your colored balls out of the circle.

▶ MODIFICATIONS

- Use beanbags instead of small balls for sliding to target.
- Use heavier, weighted balls for a slower more controlled roll.

Soccer Goals

▶ NEED AND DISABILITY

This is a game for students with and without multiple intellectual disabilities. Students with emerging skills have the chance to work on eye–hand coordination and ball skills with a portable modified goal that can be placed in any playing area. The goal can be used for multiple sports.

▶ TOOLS

Hand saw or PVC pipe cutter, tape measure

▶ SUPPLIES

Makes two complete goals.

  4 1-inch PVC pipes 10 feet long

  12 1-inch 90-degree elbow joints

  1 container of PVC pipe glue

▶ INSTRUCTIONS

1. Cut PVC into four 4-foot lengths, four 2-1/2-foot lengths, and four 2-foot lengths. (Some hardware stores will cut to order for you.)

2. Use elbow joints to assemble the pipes into two goals as shown in the diagram.

3. Leave the 4-foot pieces unglued to make it more portable.

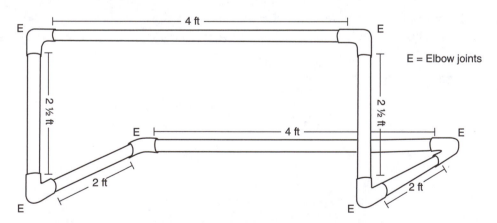

▶ IDEAS FOR USING THIS EQUIPMENT

• Use regulation soccer or hockey rules with individual modifications.

• Use a shorter playing field, 1v1 games, or 2v2 games.

• Use a bigger ball or multiple balls for various students.

• Attach hockey stick to a wheelchair to push ball around.

• Play scooter soccer.

Tinikling Bars

NEED AND DISABILITY

Tinikling bars made from PVC pipe is an inexpensive tool for all students. The added gripper makes it easier to hold. Students with emerging skills will work on tapping patterns, rhythms, agility, step patterns, and spatial awareness.

TOOLS

Hand saw or PVC pipe cutter, tape measure

SUPPLIES

> 2 1-1/2-inch PVC pipes 8 feet long
>
> 4 1-1/2-inch end caps
>
> 4 1-1/2-inch T-joints

INSTRUCTIONS

1. Cut PVC into two 6-foot lengths and two 2-foot lengths.
2. Attach T-joints to the ends of the 2-foot sections.
3. Place end caps on the ends of the 6-foot sections.

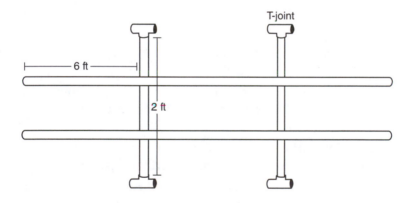

IDEAS FOR USING THIS EQUIPMENT

Teach simple movement (stepping) patterns in a routine with music. Jump up and down without hitting bars while they are moving.

MODIFICATIONS

Put grippers on ends so grasp is easier to hold on to.

Vic's Tennis Ball Foosball

▶ NEED AND DISABILITY

This game is for students of all physical abilities. Students with emerging skills can work on eye–hand coordination and sportsmanship. Foosball is a modified game that is portable and can be played on any surface. This is a great game to play on a large table or on the floor to accommodate students who are ambulatory or in wheelchairs.

▶ TOOLS

Hand saw or PVC pipe cutter, tape measure

▶ SUPPLIES

1-inch PVC pipe 32 feet long

8 1-inch end caps

26 1-inch T-joints

12 1-inch 90-degree elbow joints

2 colors of floor tape

1 container of PVC pipe glue

1 tennis ball

▶ INSTRUCTIONS

1. Cut PVC into eight 2-inch pieces, sixteen 6-inch pieces, ten 12-inch pieces, and eight 18-inch pieces.

2. Attach two pieces of the 6-inch PVC to four of the elbows. These are your corners of the game frame. Continue with remaining sideline pieces as shown in the diagram.

3. For each goal assembly, use four elbows, two 2-inch PVC pieces, and a 6-inch PVC piece. Assemble as shown in the diagram.

4. Sticks for use as strikes are as follows (for two goalkeepers and two offensive strikers; 4 players and sticks total):

   • Goalkeeper sticks: two 12-inch PVC pieces, two 6-inch PVC pieces, and three T-joints. Assemble as shown in the diagram. Repeat for the other team's goalkeeper stick.

   • Offensive strikers: one 12-inch PVC piece, two 18-inch PVC pieces, and two T-joints. Assemble as shown in the diagram. Repeat for the other team's offensive strikers sticks.

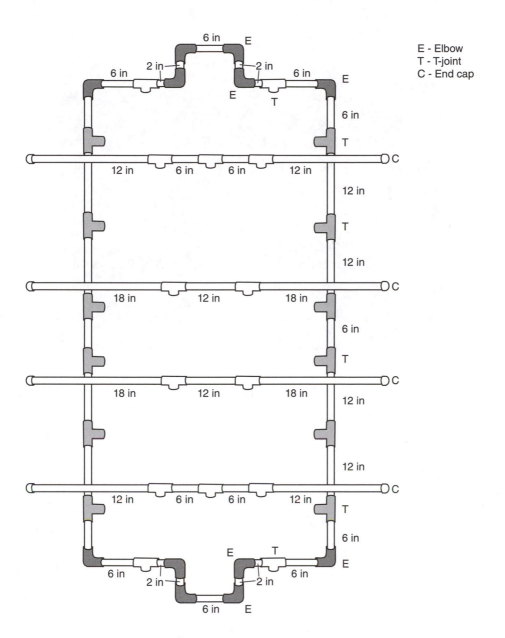

E - Elbow
T - T-joint
C - End cap

5. Glue sideline joints and endline joints, leaving the elbows at each corner removable for easy transport.

6. Mark goals and sticks with tape of two different colors to distinguish each.

(continued)

Vic's Tennis Ball Foosball   *(continued)*

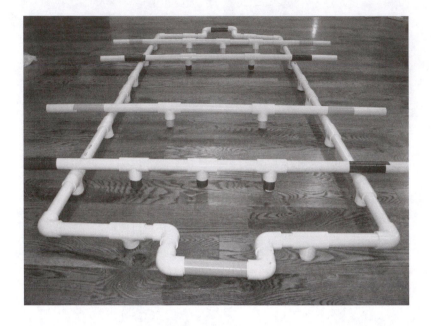

▶IDEAS FOR USING THIS EQUIPMENT

Play with two teams, using foosball rules.

Hole-in-One Target Ball

▶ NEED AND DISABILITY

This game is ideal when only a small space is available. Students of all intellectual abilities can play. Students work on throwing and catching skills and cardiorespiratory endurance. Students in wheelchairs or walkers are given the opportunity to play alongside their classmates who do not use wheelchairs or walkers.

▶ TOOLS

Scissors

▶ SUPPLIES

1 old bed sheet or shower curtain

20- to 25-foot rope

10 Softi balls or foam balls

▶ INSTRUCTIONS

1. Run the rope through the top of the sewn section of the sheet.
2. Attach rope to hooks on each side of room or tie to basketball goals in gym.
3. Cut holes in the sheet while it is hanging. Holes should be in a variety of sizes for added challenges to students.

▶ IDEAS FOR USING THIS EQUIPMENT

- Divide into two teams, each on one side with a set amount of balls. The object is to score through the holes in the sheet. This curtain can be used as a room divider.
- Use different sizes of balls or textured balls for smaller or delicate hands.
- Let students get closer to the net sheet to be successful.
- Have all students sit and throw.
- Have students stay seated at all times during play.
- Have all students use scooter boards to move around the area.

Hook 'n' Lasso Golf

▶NEED AND DISABILITY

This is a game for students of all abilities. Students with emerging skills have the opportunity to develop eye–hand coordination and ball skills. Hook 'n' lasso golf is portable and can be played in any area. This is a great game for students who are ambulatory or in wheelchairs. In addition, hook 'n' lasso golf makes a great family game and is a Texas tradition.

▶TOOLS

Hand saw or PVC pipe cutter, tape measure, drill

▶SUPPLIES

   2 1-inch pieces of PVC piping 10 feet long

   6 1-inch 90-degree elbow joints

   6 1-inch T-joints

   12 golf balls of two different colors, if possible

   6 12-inch pieces of cord of two different colors, if possible

   1 container of PVC pipe glue (optional)

▶INSTRUCTIONS

1. Cut PVC into five 2-foot lengths and ten 1-foot lengths.
2. For game base, use two 2-foot lengths and four 1-foot lengths of PVC pipe, four elbows, and two T-joints. Assemble as in the diagram.
3. For game upright piece, use three 2-foot lengths and six 1-foot lengths of PVC pipe, two elbows, and four T-joints. Assemble as in the diagram.
4. Glue the game base pieces with PVC glue and the upright piece of game with PVC glue. For easy transportation, do not glue the one joint that attaches these two pieces.
5. Drill a 1/8-inch hole through all 12 golf balls. Thread cord through balls and tie a knot to keep the ball from slipping off the cord.

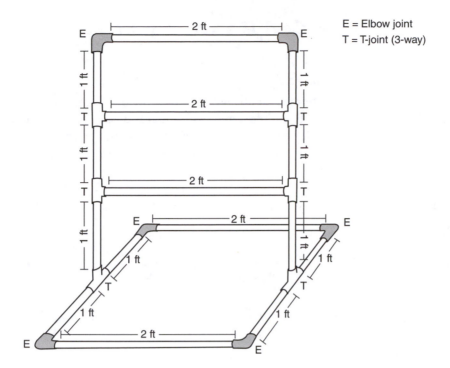

E = Elbow joint
T = T-joint (3-way)

▶IDEAS FOR USING THIS EQUIPMENT

- Play in a park or parking lot.
- Swing two balls on rope at target a minimum of 30 feet away. Award points for different bars that the rope wraps around. Points are as follows:

    Top bar: 1

    Middle bar: 2

    Bottom bar: 3

- Play each game to 20 points.
    - Shorten the game to 10 points or your choice.
    - Shorten the distance thrown.

▶MODIFICATIONS

- Use larger balls (such as tennis balls).
- Use a shorter rope between the balls or a shorter distance to throw.
- Use gripped balls to address various students' needs.

Recycled Beanbag Toss

▶ NEED AND DISABILITY

This is a game that challenges all students to toss an object at a target. The students in wheelchairs and walkers can compete alongside their ambulatory peers. Playing this game allows students to work on eye–hand coordination and ball skills. The game is also portable enough to be taken to any playing area.

▶ TOOLS

Hand saw or electric saw, screwdriver, tape measure, paint supplies

▶ SUPPLIES

Makes two complete pieces.

- 2 pieces of plywood 3 feet by 18 inches by 1/2 inch
- 4 3-inch hinges
- 2 12-inch cuts of trim board 1 inch by 2 inches by 5 inches
- 2 18-inch cuts of trim board 1 inch by 2 inches by 5 inches
- 4 trash can lids (such as from kitchen trash cans)
- 10 balls or beanbags
- Paint color of your choice

▶ INSTRUCTIONS

1. Cut out opening in the 1/2-inch plywood for trash can lids to fit inside. This measurement will vary depending on size of trash can lid. Place trash can lid on wood and trace the outline of lid for guidance.

2. Paint the plywood the color of your choice.

3. Push lid from bottom of wood up into the cutout. It must fit snugly. You might need glue or a small screw to hold lid in place.

4. Attach two 12-inch trim boards to one 18-inch trim board in a U-shape. You might need to use some sort of staple to attach the boards together.

5. Attach the U-shaped trim boards you just assembled to 1/2-inch plywood with two 3-inch hinges about 3 inches apart. See the diagram.

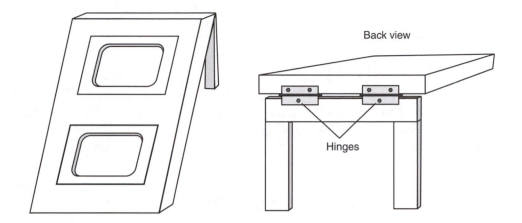

Back view

Hinges

IDEAS FOR USING THIS EQUIPMENT

- Play beanbag toss games. (Hit target to get a point; the first person to get 10 points wins.)
- Change the distance the students throw as needed to suit their abilities.

MODIFICATIONS

Use smaller or bigger balls based on students' needs.

Washers

NEED AND DISABILITY

This is a game for students of all abilities. Students with emerging skills have the opportunity to develop eye–hand coordination and ball skills. This is a portable game and is great for students who are ambulatory or in wheelchairs. In addition, washers is a great family game and a Texas tradition!

TOOLS

Hand saw or portable circular saw, tape measure

SUPPLIES

Makes two complete pieces.

2 pieces of plywood 3 feet by 18 inches by 1/2 inch

4 3-inch hinges

4 12-inch cuts of trim board 1 inch by 2 inches by 5 feet

2 18-inch cuts of trim board 1 inch by 2 inches by 5 feet

10 washers (heavy duty, such as 2-5/8 inches in diameter) in two colors

Approximately 12 square feet of AstroTurf carpet

INSTRUCTIONS

1. Cut three holes in 1/2-inch plywood approximately 3 inches in diameter and 4 inches apart, as shown in the diagram.
2. Glue AstroTurf to top of plywood. Cut into AstroTurf to expose cut hole in wood. Glue excess turf to underside of plywood.
3. Attach two 12-inch trim boards to one 18-inch trim board in a U-shape. You might need to use some sort of staple to attach the boards together.
4. Attach the U-shaped trim boards you just assembled to 1/2-inch plywood with two 3-inch hinges about 3 inches apart.

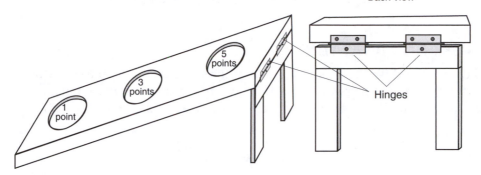

IDEAS FOR USING THIS EQUIPMENT

- Toss washers at target; receive points for hitting target. The first to reach 25 points wins.
- Modify distance washers are thrown.
- Vary the points available for each hole.

Hose Rocket (Zip-Line)

NEED AND DISABILITY

This is a modified zip-line and is a tool for students of all abilities. Students with emerging skills have the opportunity to work on strength, balance, and coordination. This is an easy activity to use with students in wheelchairs.

TOOLS

Hand saw or PVC pipe cutter, tape measure

SUPPLIES

  5 1-inch pieces of PVC piping, each 4 inches long

  1 pair of pantyhose (cut top part off; you need only the leg portion)

INSTRUCTIONS

  1. Pull pantyhose through one of the pieces of PVC pipe.
  2. Attach ends of pantyhose legs to other four pieces of PVC pipe. One piece of PVC should be able to slide back and forth.

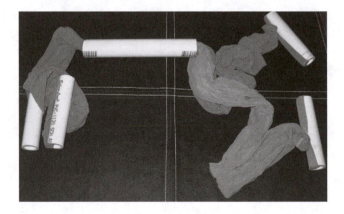

IDEAS FOR USING THIS EQUIPMENT

Partners team up in 60 seconds to count how many times they can make the pipe go back and forth.

MODIFICATIONS

  • Use bigger size of PVC pipe to allow students to grasp the handle easier.
  • Use smaller pipe to offer a greater challenge for students with higher ability.
  • Add foam to PVC pipe to allow students with grasping difficulties to independently hold handle.

Fishing

NEED AND DISABILITY

This game is great fun for students with multiple intellectual disabilities. Students with emerging skills have the opportunity to work on eye–hand coordination and manipulative skills. This game is also portable and can be played in any area. This is a great game for both ambulatory students and those in wheelchairs.

TOOLS

Tape (electrical or duct) and stapler

SUPPLIES

Magnet from discount or craft store

Bamboo stick or any household handle (such as that from a broom or mop) or yardstick

Rubber or plastic fish

INSTRUCTIONS

1. Attach a magnet to the end of a bamboo stick, long handle, or yardstick.
2. Staple through the rubber fish a couple of times; this makes the fish magnetized.

IDEAS FOR USING THIS EQUIPMENT

- Put the fish in a baby swimming pool and let students use one of the sticks to "fish."
- Bring game and fish out so that class can do a unit on fishing.
- Use different sizes or colors of fish for different point values and play a game to 20 points.
- Put up shower curtain and make it a "go fish" booth.
- Guide the students' hands to help them be successful.
- Have students work in pairs.

MODIFICATIONS

- Print pictures of fish or other animals from the computer and laminate them. Then attach paper clips or staples to the paper fish to make them magnetized.
- Supplies other than fish could be crabs or butterflies.

Table Racing

▶ NEED AND DISABILITY

This is a game for students with or without multiple intellectual disabilities. Students with emerging skills have the opportunity to work on eye–hand coordination with a modified tabletop race track.

▶ TOOLS

Hand saw or industrial scissors, tape measure

▶ SUPPLIES

    2 pieces of foam board 2 by 4 by 1/2 inches

    1 piece of AstroTurf 2 by 4 inches

    4 disposable straws

    4 lightweight Styrofoam balls or cotton balls

    Multipurpose glue

▶ INSTRUCTIONS

    1. Glue the AstroTurf to one of the foam boards.

    2. Cut out a race track from the other piece of foam board.

    3. Glue the track to the AstroTurf.

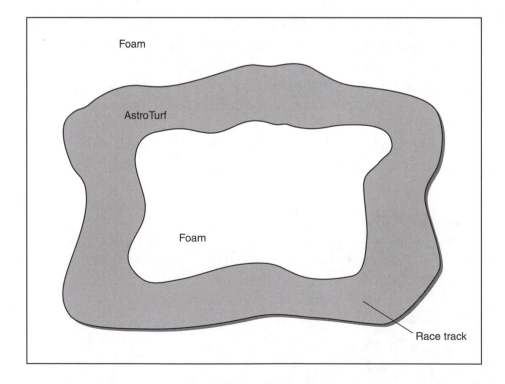

▶IDEAS FOR USING THIS EQUIPMENT

- Two people race around the board by blowing through a straw onto a Styrofoam ball. The first to finish two laps wins.
- Try remote-control cars.

▶MODIFICATIONS

- Use a big straw, which is easier to blow through.
- Place race track on lazy Suzan for students in wheelchairs.

Ring Toss

NEED AND DISABILITY

This is a game for students of all abilities. Students with emerging skills have the opportunity to work on color identification, eye–hand coordination, accuracy, and teamwork. Students in wheelchairs can play the game on a tabletop or on the floor with their peers. This game is great for fine motor activities; it can be played individually or on teams.

TOOLS

Hand saw or electric saw, electric drill (1/2-inch bit), tape measure, hammer

SUPPLIES

1 piece of plywood 1 by 18 by 24 inches

72 1/2-inch dowel rods cut into 4-inch pieces

2 trim boards 1 by 1 by 18 inches

2 trim boards 1 by 1 by 23 inches

30 store-bought small colored plastic rings approximately 2 inches in diameter

20 1/2-inch nails

1 bottle wood glue

INSTRUCTIONS

1. Mark out a grid on the piece of plywood. Marks are 2 inches apart.
2. Drill 1/2-inch holes into the plywood where you made your marks on the grid.
3. Nail trim boards to plywood around the outside edge.
4. Place one drop of wood glue into each drilled hole to secure dowel rods.
5. Place cut dowel rod pieces into each hole. You might need to tap lightly with hammer.

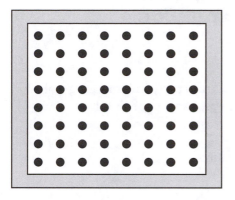 

▶IDEAS FOR USING THIS EQUIPMENT

Students throw the rings on the pegs.

▶MODIFICATIONS

Make the playing board bigger or smaller to meet individual skill levels.

Movable Ring Toss

▶ NEED AND DISABILITY

This is a game for students of all abilities. Students with emerging skills have the opportunity to work on balance and eye–hand coordination.

▶ TOOLS

Hand saw or PVC pipe cutter, tape measure

▶ SUPPLIES

1 scooter board

1 1/2-inch dowel rod 12 inches long (size of hole in scooter board would determine size of dowel rod)

1 piece of 1-inch PVC piping 8 feet long

3 1-inch T-joints

4 1-inch 90-degree elbow joints

4 1-inch end caps

1 container of PVC glue

▶ INSTRUCTIONS

1. Cut PVC pipe into one 4-foot length, six 3-inch lengths, and four 6-inch lengths.

2. Push dowel rod through hole in the middle of the scooter board.

3. Place 4-foot section of PVC over secured dowel rod. Glue can be added to dowel rod before applying PVC pipe for stability. (Some scooter boards have different-sized holes in the middle. This would determine the size of the dowel rod and the diameter of the PVC.)

4. Top section of game:
   - Attach one T-joint to top of 4-foot section.
   - Add one section of 3-inch PVC to each side of T-joint.
   - From there, add another T-joint to each section of 3-inch PVC pipe.
   - Continue with 3-inch section to elbow joint to 6-inch section to end cap.
   - Repeat this step on all four ends.

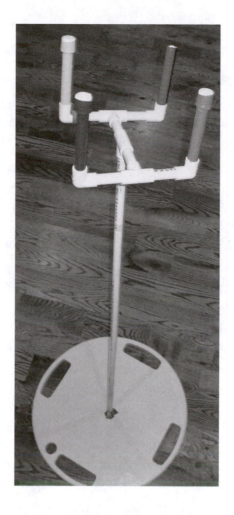

▶IDEAS FOR USING THIS EQUIPMENT

- Play a ring toss game. Players take turns throwing rings on stand.
- Throw rings onto arms as scooter passes by.

▶MODIFICATIONS

To create an easier game, you can make the stabilizing scooter board by attaching a 4-foot PVC pipe to a stationary object.

Bombs Away

▶ NEED AND DISABILITY

This is a game for those with or without physical or intellectual disabilities. Bombs away gives students the opportunity to work on eye–hand coordination, auditory response, visual stimulation, and turn-taking skills.

▶ TOOLS

Hand saw or industrial scissors, electric drill (1/4-inch bit), tape measure

▶ SUPPLIES

1 old lamp shade (size can vary; cut the hole in water container to the same size as top of lamp shade)

1 5-gallon water container

10 1/4-inch dowel rods (2-3 feet each)

30 tennis balls

1 cylinder 12 inches in diameter and 18 inches in height

Fine to medium sandpaper

Hot glue or multipurpose glue

▶ INSTRUCTIONS

1. Cut dowel rods into 12-inch lengths. Smooth off ends with sandpaper.

2. Drill 1/4-inch holes in random pattern around circumference of water container. You will need to drill more holes than dowel rods to be able to play the game.

3. Cut the bottom of 5-gallon water container to the same diameter as the small end or top of lamp shade.

4. Cut the top of water bottle (where the water would be poured out) slightly bigger than a tennis ball; you might need to make adjustments as you see the balls get stuck.

5. Place shade upside down into water container. Secure with glue.

6. Cut out opening 5 inches square in front of water container. This is used as an opening to retrieve fallen balls.

7. Place water container upside down on top of cylinder.

8. Secure water container and cylinder together with glue.

IDEAS FOR USING THIS EQUIPMENT

Push all dowel rods through holes on side of container through to other side. Once all rods are through holes, place all the tennis balls inside cylinder. Rods will hold balls until game begins.

This is much like the game Kerplunk. Students take turns strategically pulling sticks one by one. The object of the game is to pull the most sticks without allowing balls to drop. Once all sticks are pulled, count total number of sticks for each team. The team with the most sticks wins.

MODIFICATIONS

- Various sizes can be made and used with multiple sizes of balls.
- The game can be set on the floor or tabletop.

Four Up and Four Down

▶ NEED AND DISABILITY

This is a recreational game for students of all abilities. Students with emerging skills have the opportunity to work on color patterns, eye–hand coordination, game strategy, and sportsmanship. Equipment can be used for activities working on flexibility, extension, grasp and release, and crossing midline.

▶ TOOLS

Requires advanced knowledge of tools.
Hand saw or electric saw (table saw recommended), screwdriver, tape measure, electric drill (4-1/4-inch and 5-inch hole cutter, and drill press recommended), hammer, 5-inch hole cutter bit, 4-1/4-inch hole cutter bit, paint supplies

▶ SUPPLIES

1 MDF board 4 feet by 8 feet by 5/8 inches

3 pine boards 1 inch by 1 inch by 10 feet

1 pine board 1 inch by 4 inches by 8 feet

2 pine boards 2 inches by 6 inches by 8 feet

1 pine board 2 inches by 4 inches by 8 feet

8 1-inch casters

2 2-1/2-inch hinges

3-inch screws

2-inch screws

Glue

Red and blue paint

▶ INSTRUCTIONS

1. Cut two 34-by-48-inch pieces from the MDF board. The 48-inch sides will be the top and bottom of the finished project and the 34-inch sides will be the left and right ends of the finished project.

2. From the leftover MDF, use a hole cutter to cut one 4-1/4-inch disc to use as a template for your game board layout. Trace around this 4-1/4-inch disc to create the 42 holes.

3. On one 34-by-48-inch piece of MDF, measure for 42 evenly spaced holes (6 down and 7 across). Each hole will be 4-1/4-inches in diameter. There should be a 1-inch space between each hole going across and a 3/4-inch space between each hole going up and down. This should leave approximately a 4-inch border along the sides and a 1-5/8-inch border along the top and bottom.

4. Using a drill press, if available, cut out the 42 holes. If a drill press is not available, an electric drill with cutter attachments can also be used. Keep these scrap discs to be used in future projects.

5. Repeat steps 2-4 with the other 34-by-48-inch piece of MDF.

6. Cut the 1-by-1-inch boards into 8 pieces, each 34 inches long.

7. Vertically nail the 1-inch strips between the columns of your cutout circles and along each outer edge on one piece of MDF board.

8. Align the other 34-by-48-inch piece of MDF over the 1-inch strips and holes and nail and glue them together.

9. Cut the 1-by-4-inch board down so that it is 48 inches long and 2-1/4 inches wide (the same width as the game board). Once it is attached to the bottom of the game board, this will keep the game pieces in place during play.

10. Use two hinges to attach the 1-by-4-by-48-inch board to the bottom of the game board. Attach a fastener on the opposite side from the hinges to create a quick release mechanism for emptying the game board.

11. Cut the 2-by-6-inch board into two pieces, each 44 inches long. Attach one to either side of the connected MDF boards so that the 2-by-6-inch boards extend 4 inches past the MDF boards at the top and 6 inches at the bottom. Be careful not to attach the 2-by-6-inch boards to the hinged portion of the game board—it needs to swing free to release the game pieces.

12. Cut the 2-by-6-inch board into 4 pieces, each 16 inches long, and 4 pieces, each 5 inches long. Assemble them to create two 5-by-19-by-6-inch boxes (the interior dimensions of the boxes will be 2 inches wide by 16 inches long by 6 inches high).

13. From the leftover MDF, cut two 10-by-20-inch pieces and attach four casters to the bottom of each piece.

14. Attach one of the 10-by-20-inch pieces of MDF to the bottom of each box.

15. Insert the 2-by-6-inch uprights on either side of the game board into the 5-by-19-by-6-inch boxes and secure them with at least 2 3-inch screws per box to create a foot base.

16. Finishing touches:
    - Add trim boards around the edges for a clean appearance as shown in the diagram.
    - Add a top piece for a clean appearance. Cut out slits in the wood that line up with the gaps in the MDF game board so that the pieces can slide down easily.

(continued)

Four Up and Four Down   *(continued)*

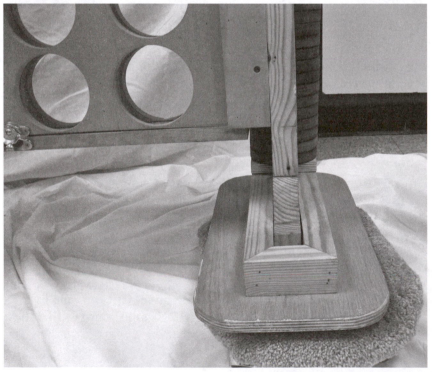

BUILD IT SO THEY CAN PLAY

17. Use the remaining MDF to cut 42 discs with a 5-inch hole cutter. These will be used as the game pieces. As you cut the game pieces, a hole will be left in the center of each one and can be used for storage (see optional step 19).

18. Paint 21 of the discs red and the other 21 blue.

19. Optional: Choose dowels that are small enough to fit through the pre-drilled holes left when the game pieces were cut out in step 17. Drill a hole the size of the dowels in each piece of scrap wood and glue the dowel in place. Attach each piece of scrap wood and dowel to the base of the game board to store game pieces.

▶ IDEAS FOR USING THIS EQUIPMENT

Much like Connect Four, this game is played by two teams: one red, one blue. The object is to get four game pieces in a row either up, down, or across.

Wonderland Board Game

NEED AND DISABILITY

This game offers auditory, visual, and tactile stimulation for students with severe or multiple intellectual disabilities. Students with emerging skills have the opportunity to work on waiting turns, one- to three-step instructions, spatial awareness, and physical fitness.

TOOLS

None needed

SUPPLIES

1 poster board approximately 24 by 36 inches

1 or 2 dice

1 black marker

1 token per player to move around board

1 tube of multipurpose glue

Random objects (from the dollar store), such as ball, bubbles, light, puppet, lotion, bell, drum, fan

Pictures of the random objects

Objects to match pictures on board

INSTRUCTIONS

1. Using the poster board as a base for the game, cut out pictures of objects you would like to add to the playing field.

2. Cut pictures to fit size of desired number of squares and glue them on the poster board.

3. Use a marker to add numbers to the board and outline the playing square borders.

4. After gluing and outlining the playing board, you can laminate the whole playing board to protect it.

5. Each square should have the object placed close by to allow for easy access during play.

▶ IDEAS FOR USING THIS EQUIPMENT

- Roll dice to move around board; complete tasks or activities.
- Students roll dice and read aloud the activity they landed on.
- Use the game on a table so wheelchairs can fit under it.

▶ MODIFICATIONS

- Make it table size, smaller, or bigger to meet your needs.
- Use various-sized dice to add to the game experience.

Modified Equipment for Sport and Recreation Activities

This chapter offers instructions on modifying equipment for a variety of sport and recreation activities. The equipment will allow all students to be active participants in any physical education and recreation setting.

PVC Bowling Ramp

▶ NEED AND DISABILITY

The PVC bowling ramp is a great tool for assisting students who cannot propel a bowling ball down the lane independently. This device would be used for students with severe intellectual and physical disabilities. This type of ramp would be used for practice purposes only.

▶ TOOLS

Hand saw or PVC cutter, tape measure

▶ SUPPLIES

> 2 1-inch PVC pipes 8 feet long
>
> 4 1-inch 90-degree elbow joints
>
> 4 1-inch T-joints
>
> 2 1-inch end caps
>
> 1 container of PVC glue

▶ INSTRUCTIONS

1. Cut the two PVC pipes into the following configurations:
   - 1 piece 2 inches long
   - 4 pieces 4 inches long
   - 2 pieces 6 inches long
   - 2 pieces 26 inches long
   - 2 pieces 5 feet long
2. Assemble as in the diagram.
3. Glue PVC at joints for better stability.

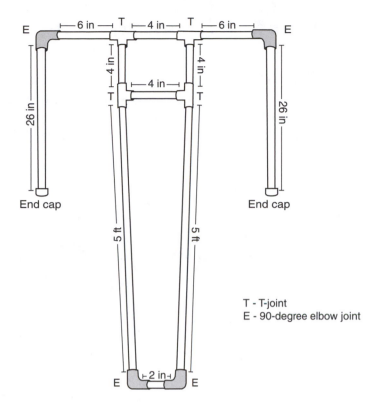

◢ IDEAS FOR USING THIS EQUIPMENT

- Use this ramp to help students propel balls down a bowling lane.
- Use this ramp for target activity games, such as knockout, where bowling pins or cones are randomly set and a student uses the ramp to aim the ball.
- Use a softer ball or lighter ball for practice in gyms.

◢ MODIFICATIONS

- Make the legs longer so wheelchairs of various heights can easily roll under.
- To help with transporting the bowling ramp, avoid gluing the key connections at the top elbow leg joint (top portions) to the ramp portion.

Wooden Bowling Ramp

▶ NEED AND DISABILITY

This is a great tool for assisting students who cannot propel bowling balls down the lane independently. Students with severe intellectual and physical disabilities would use this device for practice purposes only.

▶ TOOLS

Hand saw or electric saw, screwdriver, tape measure

▶ SUPPLIES

1 piece of wood 1 inch by 6 inches by 4 feet

2 pieces of trim wood 1 inch by 4 inches by 4 feet

8 1-1/2-inch screws

Wood glue

▶ INSTRUCTIONS

1. Attach one trim board to each side of 4-foot section of 1-by-6-inch piece of wood.
2. Reinforce the connection by applying wood glue before screwing the two pieces together.

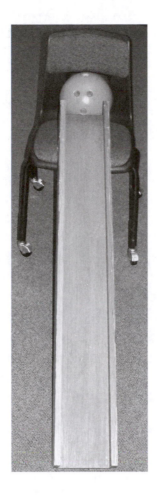

▶IDEAS FOR USING THIS EQUIPMENT

- Use this for bocce ball, practice bowling, and target ball for students in wheelchairs.
- Use foam and lighter balls.

▶MODIFICATIONS

Try making the board longer or wider, or use a material other than wood.

Hula Hoop Basketball

▶NEED AND DISABILITY

This is for students of all abilities but on a lower level of play. Using three hoops allows for three levels of difficulty. Students with emerging skills have the chance to work on eye–hand coordination, teamwork, and ball skills.

▶TOOLS

None needed

▶SUPPLIES

3 hula hoops

3 small pieces of rope or tape

▶INSTRUCTIONS

1. Attach three hula hoops together end to end using tape or rope.
2. Suspend hula hoops from regulation basketball goal by looping top hula hoop, another piece of rope, or a hook over rim of basket.

▶ MODIFICATIONS

Attach hoops to wall with either hook or tape with bottom hoop angled outward.

▶ IDEAS FOR USING THIS EQUIPMENT

Play lower-skill basketball game. Use hoops for target games or skill practice. Also, this device is great for throwing swim noodles through, as in a javelin throw.

Modified Pull-Up Bar

▶ NEED AND DISABILITY

This is a fitness tool for students of all abilities. Students with emerging skills have the opportunity to work on upper-body strength.

▶ TOOLS

Hand saw or electric saw, tape measure, hammer

▶ SUPPLIES

2 boards 2 inches by 4 inches by 4 feet

1 board 2 inches by 4 inches by 33 inches

2 boards 2 inches by 6 inches by 2-1/2 feet

1 piece of plywood 3 feet by 2-1/2 feet

1 piece of carpet or rubber matting 3-1/2 by 2-1/2 feet

1 1-inch pipe 3-1/2 feet in length, with threads on each end to put end caps on

2 1-inch end caps

4 corner brackets for stability

Wood glue

▶ INSTRUCTIONS

1. Take the 2 4-foot pieces of wood and drill 1-inch holes in both about 2 inches apart going down the wood. Make sure the holes in both boards are aligned with each other.

2. Nail 33-inch board to both of the 4-foot sections, making a U-shape. Using the corner brackets, attach at the top 90-degree angle on both sides of the structure.

3. Using wood glue and nails, attach the two 2-by-4s that are 2-1/2 feet long to the edges of the plywood.

4. Glue carpet or rubber matting to the top of the plywood, covering as much wood as possible. If you have enough carpet, you can run it up the sides.

5. Attach the U-shaped section to the base part. The 2-by-4 pieces you added to the base section should be on the inside of the U-shaped section. Attach with wood glue and nails.

6. Screw on one end cap to the pipe and slide it through one of the predrilled holes; line it up with the opposite side and push through. Secure with last end cap.

▶ IDEAS FOR USING THIS EQUIPMENT

Lie flat on the floor, extend arms, grab bar, and pull chest to bar.

Ball Drop

NEED AND DISABILITY

This is a fun tool for students of all abilities. Students with emerging skills have the opportunity to work on eye–hand coordination.

TOOLS

Hand saw or electric saw, tape measure, screwdriver

SUPPLIES

    1 6-inch PVC pipe 4 feet long

    1 90-degree hook

    1 old rolling chair
       (can be broken)

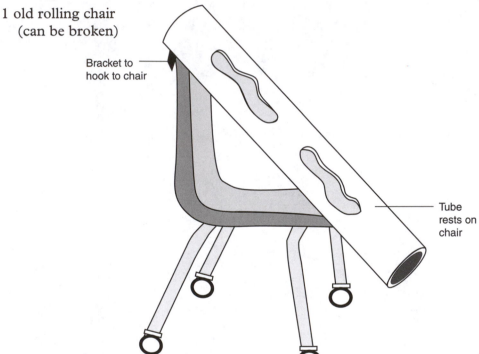

Bracket to hook to chair

Tube rests on chair

INSTRUCTIONS

1. Take PVC and attach hook approximately 8 inches from the top.

2. Hook on the top of chair.

3. An option is to cut holes in top of PVC for viewing of ball as it travels down PVC.

IDEAS FOR USING THIS EQUIPMENT

• Use as a shoot for bowling, bocce, and target games.

• Let students pull chair with them around area to retrieve and drop balls through a chute.

Shuffleboard Stick

NEED AND DISABILITY

This is a tool for students of all physical abilities. Making a shuffleboard stick is much more economical than purchasing it. Using the stick to play shuffleboard allows students to learn strategies, teamwork, and coordination. Students in wheelchairs can use this equipment alongside their peers.

TOOLS

Hand saw or PVC cutters, tape measure

SUPPLIES

1-inch PVC piping 4 feet long

1 1-inch T-joint

2 1-inch 90-degree elbow joints

3 1-inch end caps

1 container of PVC pipe glue

INSTRUCTIONS

1. Cut PVC into the following configurations:
   - 1 3-foot length
   - 4 3-inch lengths
2. Assemble as shown in the diagram.
3. Glue joints for stability and to prevent wear and tear.

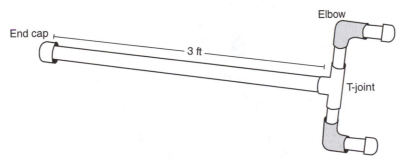

IDEAS FOR USING THIS EQUIPMENT

Play shuffleboard using the shuffleboard stick to push the puck down the playing area.

MODIFICATIONS

Make the stick longer for taller players or shorter for short players. This is a great tool for students in wheelchairs.

Duct Tape Juggling

▶ NEED AND DISABILITY

This is a tool for students of all abilities. Students with emerging skills have the opportunity to work on eye–hand coordination and a slow-motion pattern to learn and follow the art of juggling. It is beneficial for visual tracking and grasping.

▶ TOOLS

None needed

▶ SUPPLIES

Duct tape

Juggling scarves

▶ INSTRUCTIONS

Using a partial triangle shape as your guide (draw only the sides, not the bottom; see diagram), place at each corner one piece of duct tape rolled with sticky side out on a wall.

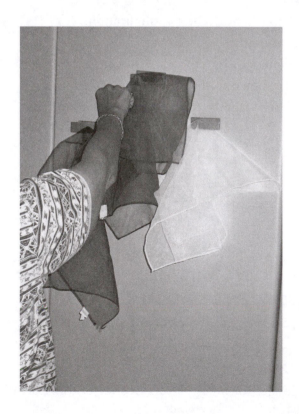

▶ IDEAS FOR USING THIS EQUIPMENT

Tacking scarves to tape allows students with slower motor functions to follow a juggling pattern. The tape holds the scarves and does not allow them to fall as they would when juggling. The scarves are tacked to the tape in a pattern and then removed according to the pattern being used (cascade or basic 1, 2, 3 pattern) depending on a student's ability level. General physical education teachers use this as a teaching station for those students who cannot get the quick sequence. For the cascade pattern, students tack juggling scarves on tape in the following sequence: With right hand holding two scarves, place one right-hand scarf to left corner, left scarf to right corner, and the second right-hand scarf to center tape (so all scarves are stuck on the wall). Depending on the student's intellectual level, he could reverse the sequence pulling down the scarf in the right corner with left hand, then use the right hand to pull the scarf in the left corner, and then the left hand to pull the scarf from the center. The student will end up with two scarves in the left hand and one scarf in the right hand. Go very slowly to teach the pattern.

▶ MODIFICATIONS

Add numbers or arrows above the tape so students can follow sequence.

Modified Jump Ropes

▶ NEED AND DISABILITY

These are tools for students with multiple intellectual and physical disabilities. Students with emerging skills work on balance and coordination with a choice of modified ropes to ensure success.

▶ TOOLS

Hand saw or PVC pipe cutter, tape measure

▶ SUPPLIES

    1 speed jump rope

    1 strip of double-sided Velcro 12 inches long

    1 hula hoop or swim noodle

    1 T-joint (depending on diameter of hula hoop)

    2 elbow joints (depending on diameter of hula hoop)

    2 small screws

    1 piece of 1/2-inch PVC pipe (different lengths to meet needs of students)

    2 washers

    1 tennis ball

    1 poly or sponge cylinder

    PVC glue and multipurpose glue

▶ INSTRUCTIONS

Modification 1

This jump rope allows students with limited use of one arm to jump a self-turning rope.

1. Remove one handle of jump rope and thread through the bottom of the PVC T-joint and knot rope so it cannot come out.
2. Thread a Velcro strip through the top PVC T-joint.
3. Attach the Velcro strip around and above the student's elbow. (The top of the T-joint is against the arm and the bottom of the T-joint faces out so the rope is free to turn.)

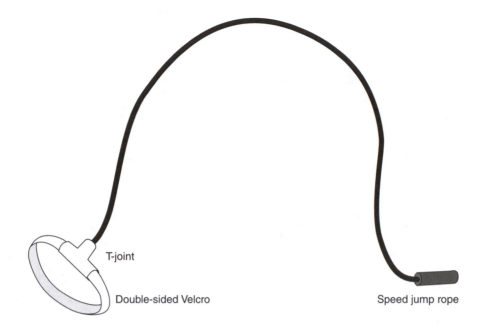

T-joint

Double-sided Velcro

Speed jump rope

Modification 2

1. Take a hula hoop and cut it at one point. This might need to be a rather large hula hoop depending on how long your PVC pipe is.

2. Attach hula hoop and PVC pipe together with small screws and glue.

3. Attach PVC pipe to elbow joints using PVC glue. Length will depend on size of hula hoop when it is expanded to desired arc.

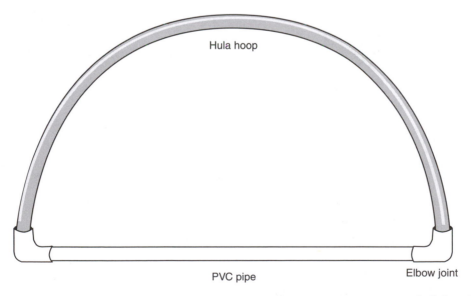

Hula hoop

PVC pipe

Elbow joint

(continued)

Modification 3

Put an ordinary speed jump rope or link rope through a hula hoop or a swim noodle. This keeps the arc of the jump rope. It also helps slow down the rope and gives a visual representation along with the weight and sound.

1. Take off one handle of jump rope.
2. Cut hula hoop to desired length (depending on size and ability of student).
3. Thread jump rope through hula hoop.
4. Reattach handle of jump rope.

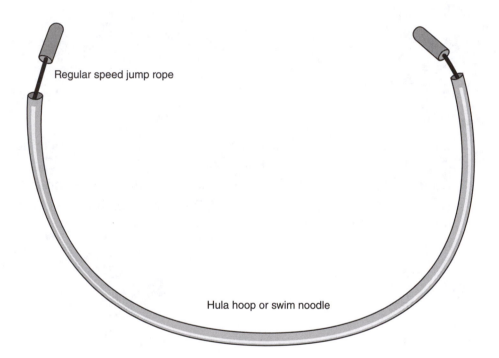

Regular speed jump rope

Hula hoop or swim noodle

Modification 4

1. Cut an ordinary speed jump rope approximately 12 to 15 inches from the handles, making sure to leave the handles intact.
2. At the end of the cut section, make a knot in the rope or thread rope through a thick washer and knot it on the end.
3. Take two tennis balls and cut two 1-inch slits on opposite sides of each ball.
4. Slip end of knot and washer into the ball. This will give students the sense of turning a jump rope.

5. Make a complete speed rope with tennis balls on each side:
   a. With the remaining rope, attach washers to ends and secure with knot.
   b. Connect speed rope to the two balls by inserting washers into tennis balls.

Tennis ball
with
washer inside

▶ IDEAS FOR USING THIS EQUIPMENT

- Students may use these modified jump ropes the same ways a regular jump rope might be used.
- Make a ladder chart of skills for students (such as 1 foot, scissor kick, high kick, front and back).

Monster Truck

NEED AND DISABILITY

This device provides students with an opportunity to experience movement skills and activities alongside their peers in physical education classes. This modified piece of equipment is for students who might have birth defects such as phocomelia or amelia. (Phocomelia is a congenital malformation, or birth defect, in which the hands and feet are attached to shorter-than-average arms and legs. Amelia is an extremely rare birth defect marked by the absence of one or more limbs.)

TOOLS

None needed

SUPPLIES

- 2 attachable scooter boards (size depends on each student's body size)
- 1 basket or plastic crate
- 1 seat cushion
- 1 foam pipe or swim noodle
- 4 small bungee cords

INSTRUCTIONS

1. Attach the basket to one scooter using one bungee cord for each corner.
2. Loop bungee cord around each wheel to secure basket.
3. Attach the two scooters together.
4. Once basket and scooters are attached and secured, place seat cushion in basket.
5. Measure and cut foam to fit around the top of the basket to soften the edge of the basket.

▶IDEAS FOR USING THIS EQUIPMENT

- Use for all types of physical education activities.
- Use for relay races.

▶MODIFICATIONS

- Use large scooters.
- Use larger basket.
- Use extra seat cushions to increase height.

Hockey Stick and Puck

▶ NEED AND DISABILITY

These are modified tools for students with or without multiple intellectual disabilities and especially beneficial for students in wheelchairs. Students with emerging skills have the opportunity to compete on the same level with their peers.

▶ TOOLS

Hand saw or PVC pipe cutter, tape measure

▶ SUPPLIES

1 piece of 1-inch PVC piping 7 feet long

2 1-inch 45-degree joints

1 1-inch 90-degree elbow joint

1 regular floor hockey puck

1 heavy-duty washer

1 Wiffle ball cut in half

Tape

PVC glue and multipurpose glue

▶ INSTRUCTIONS

Stick

1. Cut PVC into the following configurations:
   - 1 3-foot length
   - 2 1-1/2-foot lengths
   - 1 1-foot length
2. Attach as in the diagram.
3. Glue for stability while playing activity.

Puck

1. Glue washer to bottom of hockey puck.
2. With tape or glue, attach half of Wiffle ball to the top of the hockey puck.

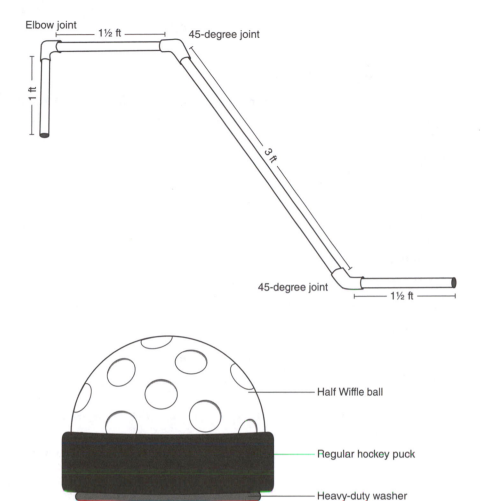

Elbow joint

1½ ft

45-degree joint

1 ft

3 ft

45-degree joint

1½ ft

Half Wiffle ball

Regular hockey puck

Heavy-duty washer

▶ IDEAS FOR USING THIS EQUIPMENT

Use regulation hockey rules with modifications for individual students. Object of game is to use hockey stick to get puck into the goal.

▶ MODIFICATIONS

- The handle fits over the brake handle on most wheelchairs. For students with limited grip, Velcro can be placed on handle and a glove if needed.
- Place foam over blade for soccer; this keeps the ball from going over the blade. Use a 6-inch sphere and drill a hole in the middle to slide blade through.

Scooter Chair

NEED AND DISABILITY

This tool gives students with severe and multiple intellectual disabilities a more stable and secure way to move on a scooter board. That way, they are able to play and participate with the class.

TOOLS

Screwdriver, electric drill (1/2-inch bit)

SUPPLIES

1 old scooter board

1 old school chair

1 safety strap (can be old belt or old seat belt)

4 1/4-inch nuts and bolts with washers

INSTRUCTIONS

1. Drill four ¼-inch holes in school chair and scooter board. Make sure to line up the holes drilled.
2. After drilling the four holes, line the chair and scooter up so holes match, push bolt with washer through holes, and attach with nut from underneath scooter.
3. Safety straps can hold a student in the chair while the activity is in progress.

IDEAS FOR USING THIS EQUIPMENT

Use in relays, scooter games, or any activity that requires scooter boards.

MODIFICATIONS

- Add another scooter board under a student's feet to raise the feet off the floor. This way they could be pushed around by a peer or assistant during activity.
- Connect two scooter boards by using a 1-by-2-inch scrap piece of wood. Cut the wood to desired length and attach to scooters by screwing the piece of wood directly into the bottom of both scooter boards.
- Use a different type of chair, such as an adult-sized chair or booster seat.

Modified Equipment for Vestibular and Fine Motor Activities

This chapter offers instructions on modifying and making equipment to enhance students' vestibular and fine motor development. Young people who need vestibular development lack body control in their dynamic and static balance, which then shows up in their locomotor patterns and sport skills. Once a student's gross motor skills are developed then their fine motor skills will benefit. All students who participate in general physical education or an adapted physical education program can benefit from using modified equipment. We will show you ideas on making the needed modifications so the students will be active participants in any activity in a general physical education setting. Equipment is cost effective, easy to make, and portable enough to be used in any learning environment. The following pages give you the tools for creating equipment that will inspire students to participate in the activities.

Combination Lock Trainer

▶NEED AND DISABILITY

This is excellent for students of all abilities. Students with emerging skills will work on eye–hand coordination. The combination lock trainer helps students learn how to use a combination lock for their lockers.

▶TOOLS

Scissors, tape measure

▶SUPPLIES

1 sheet of card stock 8 by 11 inches

3 brads

▶INSTRUCTIONS

1. Cut the card stock in half lengthwise.
2. Cut three circles approximately 3 inches in diameter out of one half of the card stock.
3. Using the brads, attach the circles to the first half of card stock about 1/2 inch apart.
4. Make a knob by cutting three smaller circles about 2 inches in diameter out of the extra card stock. Cut slits in them and fold the sides under to make a knob.
5. Attach with tape or glue.
6. Mark the numbers around the edges of the bigger circle and then label the directions and combination. See the diagram.

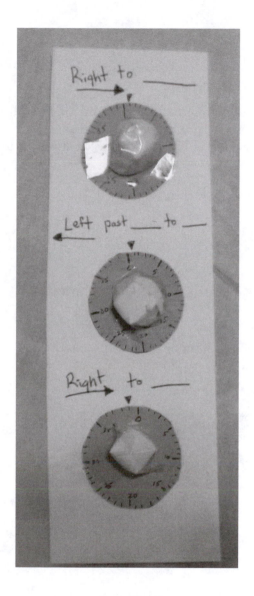

▶ IDEAS FOR USING THIS EQUIPMENT

This is a great trainer for those students who are having a difficult time with their combination locks. Once they are successful with the trainer, try old locks until they are successful then try it in the actual locker room.

Tug-a-Play

NEED AND DISABILITY

This is a strength-developing tool for students of all abilities. Students with emerging skills have the opportunity to work on strength, balance, and coordination. Tug-a-play can easily be modified for students in wheelchairs.

TOOLS

Hand saw and electric drill (1/4-inch bit), tape measure

SUPPLIES

2 2-inch dowel rods 12 inches long

10-foot rope

1 object to tie in middle (scarf, ribbon, or just a knot in the rope)

INSTRUCTIONS

1. Drill a hole through both of the dowel rods.
2. Push end of rope through hole and tie knot.
3. Attach the object to the middle of the rope.

IDEAS FOR USING THIS EQUIPMENT

Each student playing holds one end of the rope. Students face each other. On the command of go, each student begins to wind up the rope, pulling against the other person. The student who reaches the middle first wins. Time them to see how quickly they can roll it up.

MODIFICATIONS

- Put PVC pipe around dowel rod and have student hold the stick; the PVC pipe will just turn.
- Attach the dowel rod to a wheelchair so the student can be the holder of the stick for the other student.

Vestibular Board

NEED AND DISABILITY

This tool offers visual and tactile stimulation for students with mild to moderate intellectual disabilities. Students with emerging skills have the opportunity to work on balance reactions, vestibular stimulation, and spatial orientation. The movement of the board allows for motor planning by encouraging students to maintain an upright stance.

TOOLS

Electric saw, tape measure, paint supplies (optional)

SUPPLIES

1 piece of MDF or plywood 2 feet by 2 feet by 1/2 inch

1 balance disc (can be purchased)

Paint (optional)

INSTRUCTIONS

1. Cut 24-inch circle out of MDF or plywood.
2. Paint a bright color if desired.
3. The balance disc is not attached; it can be used for raising level of difficulty.

IDEAS FOR USING THIS EQUIPMENT

Use the discs for balance activities. Here are examples:

- Partners hold hands; one stands on disc and one is on floor for stability.
- Both partners stand on a disc, holding hands for support.
- Stand on one foot on disc.
- Do squats or leg lifts while on disc.
- Do basketball skills such as dribbling or passing with partner.
- Stand on the balance disc while lifting light hand weights.

Big Foot

NEED AND DISABILITY

This is an activity for students of all abilities. Students with emerging skills have the opportunity to work on balance and coordination with modified stepping shoes. There are two options: working on stepping independently and working with partners as a cooperative effort.

TOOLS

Hand saw or electric saw, tape measure, glue, electric drill (1/2-inch bit)

SUPPLIES

2 1/2-inch boards 14 by 8 inches

2 pieces of old foam

8-foot rope (longer rope might be needed for taller students to use stepping shoes)

INSTRUCTIONS

1. Cut the boards into shape of choice. Square, rectangle, and circle are options.
2. On each side of the shape, drill two holes from the top to the bottom.
3. Use 6-inch piece of rope to loop through each set of holes you drilled. Repeat on second shoe.

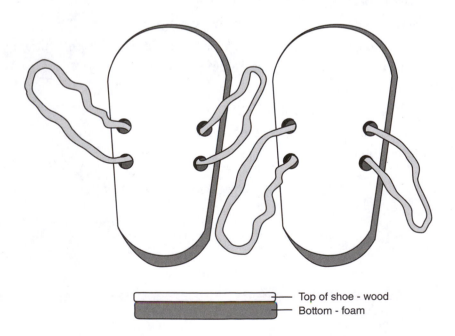

Top of shoe - wood
Bottom - foam

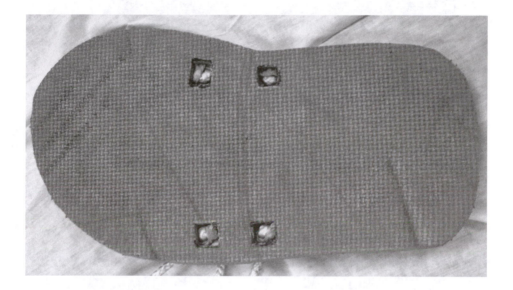

4. Take remaining 6 feet of rope and cut in half. Tie one end to each 6-inch section of rope on one shoe. Repeat with the other half of the rope on second shoe.

5. Cut out the same shape of foam. Don't forget to cut out holes where the rope comes through the wood.

6. Glue soft foam to bottom of wood for cushion.

▶ IDEAS FOR USING THIS EQUIPMENT

- Students use one foot to practice and understand the movement. This movement teaches students to pick up their feet when they walk.

- Work on coordination, balance, and patterns. Use as a station in obstacle course or for relays.

Cooperative Walking Boards

▶NEED AND DISABILITY

This is an activity for students of all abilities. Students with emerging skills have the opportunity to work on balance and coordination with modified stepping shoes. There are two options: working on stepping independently and working with partners as a cooperative effort.

▶TOOLS

Electric drill (1/2-inch bit)

▶SUPPLIES

2 pieces of pine wood 1 inch by 6 inches by 6 feet

2 12-foot sections of rope

4 handles (PVC pipe or other) 5 inches long

8 washers

▶INSTRUCTIONS

1. Drill one hole about 12 inches from each end of the boards (total of two holes per board).
2. Cut each rope into two equal sections, approximately 6 feet per section, for a total of four pieces.
3. Run one piece of rope through one hole with a washer on each side of the board to ensure that the rope won't slip.
4. Tie off the rope on the underside of board, ensuring the washer is snug to the board.
5. Tie off rope on top side of board, ensuring the washer is snug to the board.
6. At the top of the rope, slide PVC handle onto rope and tie off rope so handle does not slip off.
7. Repeat for second rope on first board.
8. Repeat all steps for second board.

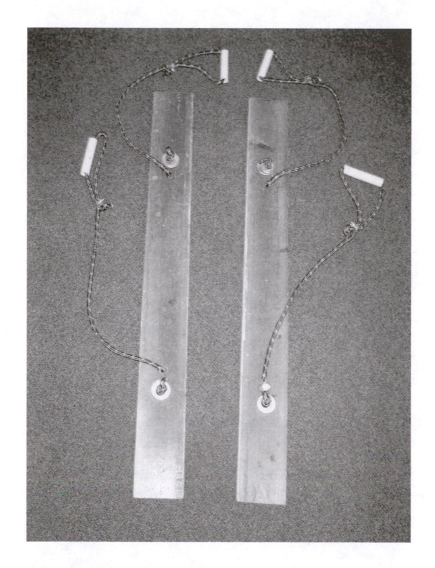

▶ IDEAS FOR USING THIS EQUIPMENT

Use in cooperative games such as walking activities and relays.

▶ MODIFICATIONS

Make with heavier wood to work on weight resistance.

Up-and-Down Board

▶ NEED AND DISABILITY

This is an activity for students of all abilities. Students with emerging skills will work on balance, eye–hand coordination, visual tracking, response, timing, and perception.

▶ TOOLS

Hand saw or electric saw, screwdriver, hammer, tape measure

▶ SUPPLIES

    1 piece of pine wood 1 by 5-1/2 by 28 inches
    1 2-inch PVC pipe 5-1/2 inches long
    1 piece of pine wood 1 by 2 by 5½ inches
    1 cylinder for placement of objects
    1 box 1/2-inch screws
    1 box 1/2-inch nails
    2 pieces of soft foam or rubber 5 by 5 inches
    1 cylinder-type cup
    1 can of indoor/outdoor paint of your choice

▶ INSTRUCTIONS

1. Nail 1-by-2-by-5-1/2-inch board to bottom of 28-inch board approximately 8 to 9 inches from one end.
2. Cut PVC pipe in half lengthwise.
3. Attach PVC to the bottom of 28-inch board by screwing into trim piece added in step 1.
4. Screw one piece of soft foam or rubber to the bottom of each end of the 28-inch board; this will help cut down on the noise when it is used.
5. Paint board a bright color if desired.
6. Using two 1/2-inch screws, attach cylinder-type cup to top of 28-inch board at opposite end of PVC (on bottom). This will assist in holding a large or small ball while attempting to stomp and catch.

▶ IDEAS FOR USING THIS EQUIPMENT

- Use in obstacle course or station activity. A student places the object on the cylinder and stomps the end of the board, catching object in the air.
- Help student set object on board.
- Use a bigger ball or object so the student is successful in catching the object.

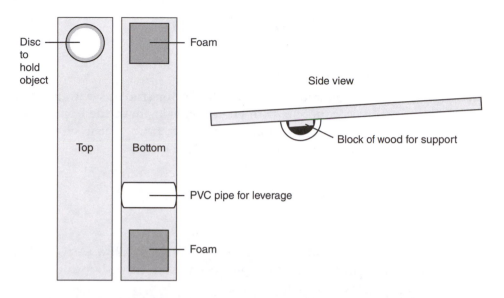

Disc to hold object

Foam

Top

Bottom

Side view

Block of wood for support

PVC pipe for leverage

Foam

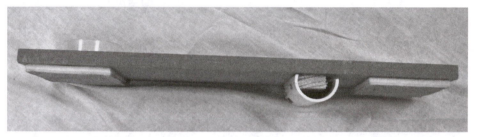

- You could stomp on board for the student and let the student catch the object.
- You could let student stomp on the board and you or a partner catch the object.
- As a baseball lead-up, pop ball up and catch with glove.

▶MODIFICATIONS

Length, width, height, and number of each beam can vary depending on the need.

Washtub Fun

NEED AND DISABILITY

This activity offers visual and tactile stimulation for students with multiple intellectual disabilities. Students with emerging skills have the opportunity to work on balance and coordination. Turn the washtub over to change the activity to one that works on manipulative skills.

TOOLS

Electric drill (1/4-inch bit), tape measure

SUPPLIES

6 plastic square or round washtubs (large enough to allow stepping in it and sturdy enough to allow stepping on it when turned upside down)

15 feet of rope at least 1 inch in diameter

1 roll spongy drawer liner

INSTRUCTIONS

1. Drill two holes on each side of tubs directly across from each other at the tops (holes should be no larger than width of rope).
2. Cut rope into 5 pieces, each 3 feet in length (melt ends so the ropes do not unravel).
3. Use the ropes to connect the tubs to each other; tie knots through holes.
4. Using the bottom of the outside of tubs, trace drawer liner and cut to glue on bottom of tubs to prevent slipping.

▶ IDEAS FOR USING THIS EQUIPMENT

- Fill the tub with various textures, such as bubble wrap or sandpaper, or fill with sudsy water. Let students feel the textures and objects inside.
- Students walk the stepping tubs in an obstacle course.
- Turn tubs upside down so students can walk the tubs for balance activity.
- Play follow the leader or Simon says. Reinforce turn-taking, waiting, and listening skills.

Stepping Stones

▶NEED AND DISABILITY

These are tools for those with mild to moderate levels of disability. Using the stepping stones gives students the opportunity to work on balance and coordination while learning cooperative play.

▶TOOLS

Industrial scissors

▶SUPPLIES

Unlimited number of flat or semiflat worn-out balls such as basketballs or soccer balls (better with heavier balls)

▶INSTRUCTIONS

Cut flat balls in half and use as stepping stones.

▶IDEAS FOR USING THIS EQUIPMENT

- Play tag while staying on stones (safe when on stones).
- Use for balance activities.
- Balance on stepping stones and throw objects to others.

▶MODIFICATIONS

Use pictures of balls or other items printed on paper or flat objects.

Moon Rocks

NEED AND DISABILITY

These are objects for those with mild to moderate levels of disabilities. Students have the opportunity to work on balance and coordination. The various difficulty levels offer a challenging learning experience.

TOOLS

Portable circular saw, ruler, tape measure, sandpaper, paint supplies

SUPPLIES

1 piece of MDF or plywood 4 by 8 feet by 1/2 inches

Multiple colors of paint

Wood glue

INSTRUCTIONS

1. Draw a rock shape approximately 3 by 5 inches on the MDF board.
2. After cutting out the shape, use a ruler to mark the distance from original shape to make a shape that is 3/4 inch bigger all the way around.
3. Continue measuring and cutting, making the shape 3/4 inch bigger every time.
4. Glue pieces together, sand with sandpaper, and paint a variety of colors.
5. Make rock shapes in a variety of heights. The height of the rocks can be altered depending on how many layers you glue together. The higher you go the more challenging it will be for the students.

IDEAS FOR USING THIS EQUIPMENT

Use in obstacle courses. Lay out moon rocks in various patterns to challenge students to complete the course while maintaining balance.

Balance Boards

NEED AND DISABILITY

These are tools for students with mild to moderate disabilities. Students maintain bodily control without stepping off. Balance boards encourage weight shifting, balance reactions, and motor planning.

TOOLS

Hand saw or electric saw, tape measure, screwdriver, hammer

SUPPLIES

1 piece of wood 1 by 12 by 24 inches

1 4-inch PVC pipe 12 inches long

1 piece of wood 1 by 2 by 12 inches

1 box of ½-inch screws

1 box of ½-inch nails

INSTRUCTIONS

1. Cut PVC in half lengthwise.
2. Nail the 1-by-2-by-12-inch piece of wood to middle of 24-inch piece of wood.
3. Using screws, attach half of PVC to 1-by-2-by-12-inch piece of wood.
4. See the diagram.
5. Flip board over to use.

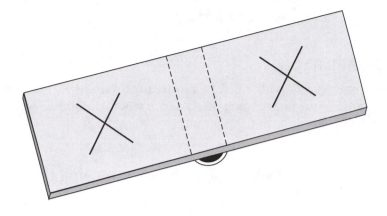

Block of wood
for support   PVC cut in half

▶ IDEAS FOR USING THIS EQUIPMENT

- While on boards, students can play catch with any kind of ball. Object is to maintain balance.
- Use as tilt board in an obstacle course.
- Use the device to rock back and forth, which promotes vestibular stimulation.
- Hold a partner's hand.
- Use a chair for stability.

Balance Stools

NEED AND DISABILITY

These are tools for students with mild to moderate disabilities. Students maintain bodily control without stepping off. Balance stools encourage weight shifting, balance reactions, and motor planning.

TOOLS

Hand saw or electric saw, portable circular saw, screw saw, drill (1/4-inch bit), tape measure

SUPPLIES

1 piece of MDF or plywood at least 15 by 15 by 1/2 inch

1 piece of 3-inch PVC 16 inches long

1 piece of 1-1/2-inch PVC 14 inches long

1 2-1/4-inch bolt with wing nut

1 1-1/2-inch rubber stopper

1 3-inch PVC coupling

1 box 1/2-inch screws

INSTRUCTIONS

1. Cut a 14-inch circle out of plywood or MDF.
2. Attach a 3-inch PVC coupling to the middle of the plywood.
3. Drill a hole through both sides of the 3-inch PVC at least 2 inches from one end.
4. Attach 3-inch PVC to the coupling already affixed to the coupling. Make sure to secure at the opposite side from where you drilled a hole.
5. Take 1-1/2-inch PVC pipe piece and drill three or four 1/4-inch holes going through and down both sides approximately 1/2 inch apart.
6. Attach the rubber stopper to the smaller of the two PVC pipes.
7. Place the 1-1/2-inch PVC pipe up into the 3-inch PVC pipe. Pipes should be able to slide back and forth to height adjustments.
8. Using the bolt and wing nut, push bolt through the desired-height holes and secure with the wing nut.

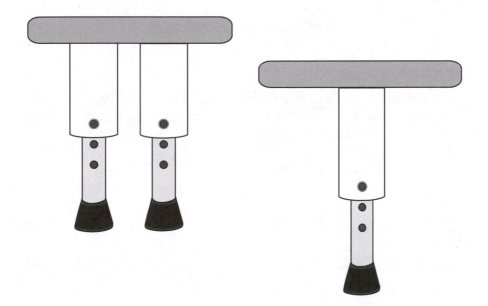

IDEAS FOR USING THIS EQUIPMENT

Have timed balance contests or stations.

MODIFICATIONS

Construct two legs for more stability. Supplies will double. Instructions are the same except you will need to place two lengths of PVC side by side, so it will not be in the middle as original instructions state.

Balance Beams

NEED AND DISABILITY

This is a tool for developing dynamic balance for students with mild to moderate intellectual disabilities. Students with emerging balance skills have the opportunity to work on balance reactions, vestibular stimulation, and spatial orientation. The portable beam allows for motor planning by encouraging students to maintain an upright stance.

TOOLS

Hand saw or electric saw, sandpaper, electric drill (1-inch bit), tape measure, router (optional)

SUPPLIES

4 hardwood planks 1 inch by 4 inches by 5 feet

1 cedar post 2 feet long or scrap blocks of wood

1 1-inch dowel rod 36 inches long

1 bottle of wood glue

INSTRUCTIONS

1. Cut cedar posts into four 6-inch-high blocks.
2. Drill two 1-inch holes 2 inches deep and 2 inches apart in center of top of the block of wood.
3. Cut dowel rod into eight 3-inch pieces.
4. Glue one dowel rod in each drilled hole leaving 1 inch sticking out. This provides a support for the beam.
5. Use router to round all edges of hardwood planks.
6. Drill one 1-inch hole on each end of the hardwood planks 2 inches from the ends.
7. Boards can now be placed in connecting square or remain in a running line.

IDEAS FOR USING THIS EQUIPMENT

- Students walk across boards to work on balance skills. This can be used in obstacle courses or as hurdles.
- Change layout of the boards to challenge students' abilities.

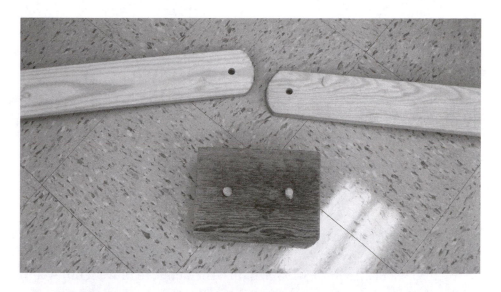

Giant Beads

▶ NEED AND DISABILITY

These tools are for students with moderate to severe disabilities. Working with the giant beads allows students to work on fine motor skills, eye–hand coordination, color identification, and crossing the midline.

▶ TOOLS

Industrial scissors, tape measure, lighter

▶ SUPPLIES

Hollow noodles in various colors (swim noodles are available at swim supply stores)

1-inch rope cut into 3- to 5-foot lengths (melt ends to prevent unraveling)

Old jump rope handles

▶ INSTRUCTIONS

1. Tie jump rope handle on one end of rope.
2. Cut noodles into various lengths: 1, 2, 5 inches, and so on.
3. Students can now thread beads onto rope.

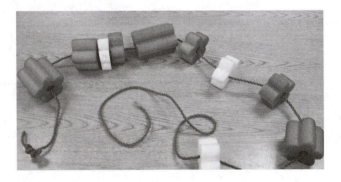

▶ IDEAS FOR USING THIS EQUIPMENT

- This activity encourages stringing experiences. This is great for eye–hand coordination and color-identification skills.
- String and unstring to create various color patterns, sizes, and shapes.
- Use as game pieces in games. Tie around the waist for chase or tag games.

▶ MODIFICATIONS

Use sponges or plastic scrub brushes instead of noodles.

Peg Boards

NEED AND DISABILITY

This tool offers visual and tactile stimulation for students with severe or multiple intellectual disabilities. Students with emerging skills have the opportunity to work on eye–hand coordination and motor planning by following patterns, colors, and sequences.

TOOLS

Hand saw or electric saw, electric drill (1/2-inch bit), tape measure, paint supplies

SUPPLIES

1 wood board 2 by 6 by 24 inches

3 or 4 1/2-inch dowel rods 36 inches long

Multiple colors of paint

INSTRUCTIONS

1. Drill 1/2-inch holes into board with at least 1/4 inch between each hole. You can do a pattern if desired. Line the holes up in rows, and create sections by painting each section a different color.

2. Cut the dowel rods into lengths varying from 2 to 4 inches. Paint each dowel piece for the colors chosen.

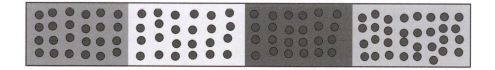

Side view

Pegs

IDEAS FOR USING THIS EQUIPMENT

Make it a ring toss, sorting game, or fine motor activity. Students will toss rings on pegs.

MODIFICATIONS

Make a bigger board, use more pegs, or paint different colors.

Giant Ring Slide Stand

NEED AND DISABILITY

This tool offers students with moderate to severe disabilities visual tracking skills needed for everyday activities. These skills include color recognition and crossing the midline. The giant ring slide stand can also aid students with standing, balance, and vestibular training. All of these skills give students a chance to be successful and have fun while learning.

TOOLS

Hand saw or PVC cutter, tape measure

SUPPLIES

1 piece of 2-inch PVC piping 12 feet long

2 2-inch 90-degree elbow joints

2 2-inch T-joints

4 2-inch end caps

6 to 8 deck rings of various colors

INSTRUCTIONS

1. Cut PVC into the following configurations:
   - four 1-foot lengths
   - one 2-foot length
   - two 2- or 3-foot lengths
2. Assemble standing rack as shown in the diagram.
3. Put on deck rings before connecting pipes.
4. Joints can be glued if desired. Leave them unglued for easy transport.
5. The stand can now be used as a ring slide game. Move pieces from one side to another.

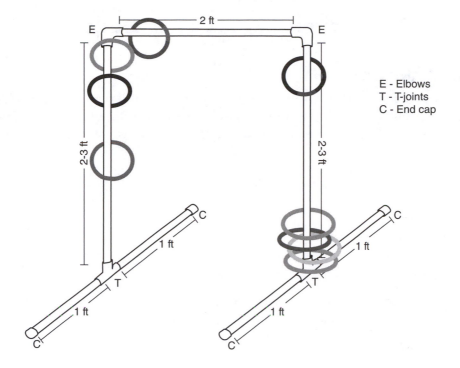

2 ft

E E

E - Elbows
T - T-joints
C - End cap

2-3 ft

2-3 ft

C C

1 ft 1 ft

T T

1 ft 1 ft

C C

▶IDEAS FOR USING THIS EQUIPMENT

This piece of equipment encourages students to cross the midline, gain control in standing and squatting, identify colors, and work on verbal skills. Hang rings from the stand, use a target, or use it as a timed event.

▶MODIFICATIONS

Make joints detachable and change objects to be moved around. Wrap PVC pipe with string or yarn for texture.

Action and Reaction Board

NEED AND DISABILITY

This is a tool for students with severe intellectual disabilities. Students with emerging skills have the opportunity to work on eye–hand coordination; auditory, tactile, and visual stimulation; and simple one- or two-step instructions.

TOOLS

Hand saw or electric saw, screwdriver, tape measure

SUPPLIES

1 peg board 2 by 4 feet

1 trim board 1 inch by 2 inches by 12 feet

3 brackets

12 big switches (recordable voice output devices)

2 step-by-steps (multiple-step voice output devices)

24 1-inch bolts

1 box trim nails

INSTRUCTIONS

1. Cut two 1-foot 11-1/2-inch lengths and two 4-foot lengths of trim board.

2. Using trim nails, attach trim pieces to the back of peg board around perimeter.

3. Attach brackets to back of trim board. This will allow you to hang it from a classroom chalk or white board while propping it on the eraser edge for extra support.

4. Attach the switches and step-by-step using two 1-inch bolts per switch from the back of the peg board. Switches should be spread apart to cover all of the peg board.

IDEAS FOR USING THIS EQUIPMENT

Use for color identification, number recognition, money applications, fitness activities, and quiz games. Two activities are shown here.

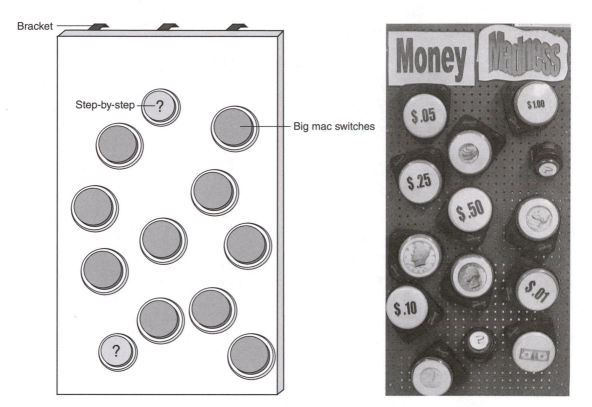

Bracket

Step-by-step

Big mac switches

Money Madness

▶ INSTRUCTIONS

Using the step-by-steps on the board, a student pushes the button. As a question is asked of the student, he or she must find the answer on the board. As the student pushes a button for the answer, the response from the big switches could be "Great job," a simple statement of the answer, or the magical sound of "yippee." You can place the step-by-step on a student's desk to allow that student to become the facilitator of the lesson.

▶ PICTURES ON BUTTONS

Dollar bill
Half dollar
Quarter
Dime
Nickel
Penny

(continued)

Action and Reaction Board *(continued)*

▶ QUESTIONS FOR THE CLASS: LOW ABILITY

- I'm a quarter; how much am I?
- I'm a dollar; how much am I?
- I'm a nickel; how much am I?
- I'm a dime; how much am I?
- I'm a half dollar; how much am I?
- I'm a penny; how much am I?
- Which coin is worth 10 cents?
- Which coin is worth 5 cents?
- Which coin is worth 25 cents?
- Which one is worth 1 dollar?
- Which coin is worth 10 cents?
- Which coin is worth 50 cents?
- Which coin is worth the least?
- Which coin is worth the most?
- Which coin is the smallest in size?
- Which coin is the biggest in size?
- Which coin is a different color than the rest?
- Which one is not a coin at all?

▶ TEXT ON BUTTONS

- $ 1.00
- $ .50
- $ .25
- $ .10
- $ .05
- $ .01

▶ QUESTIONS FOR THE CLASS: HIGHER ABILITY

- How much do 2 quarters equal?
- How much do 2 half dollars equal?
- How much do 2 dimes and 1 nickel equal?
- How much do 5 pennies equal?
- How much do 5 nickels equal?
- How much is 1 dollar minus 50 cents?

- How much is 50 cents minus 25 cents?
- How much is 25 cents minus 15 cents?
- How much is 1 dime minus a nickel?
- How much is 10 cents minus 5 pennies?
- 2 of what adds up to 50 cents?
- 5 of what adds up to a nickel?
- 10 of what adds up to 1 dollar?
- 2 of what adds up to a dollar?
- 4 of what adds up to a dollar?
- 5 of what adds up to 50 cents?
- 10 of what adds up to a dime?
- 100 of what adds up to 1 dollar?

Sully Says: Colors

▶ COLOR OF BUTTONS

Red

Blue

Green

Yellow

Orange

Purple

Brown

Black

▶ RECORDED ON BIG SWITCHES

Orange

Purple

Brown

Blue

Black

Red

Green

Yellow

(continued)

Action and Reaction Board   *(continued)*

▶RECORDED ON STEP-BY-STEP

Using the step-by-step, record the same colors you have on the big switches. Put the recorded colors in a different order for each one. This way the loop will be disrupted every time a student pushes a step-by-step.

▶INSTRUCTIONS

A student starts by pushing any switch. The student is then prompted to go to the next color and push the switch which will prompt the student to go to the next color or switch. This will continue until you stop the activity. Learning colors is just one way to use this game. Time the students to make it a reaction game determining how many correct switches they can hit in a set time.

▶MODIFICATIONS

Call out a color; the student has to find the color. If you do this type of activity, you must reprogram the buttons to say, "Correct," or "Good job." Or you could have a sound recorded on it.

Sensory Equipment

This chapter offers instructions on setting up a sensory motor lab and building sensory equipment to be used in a variety of settings. It targets students with multiple mild to severe disabilities for whom the general physical education setting is not the most appropriate. These activities are geared toward but not limited to students who cannot grasp objects and whose level of play is far below that of their peers.

Developing a program for this population of students can be difficult. This chapter presents ideas for auditory, visual, and tactile stimulation for students with sensorimotor problems. For example, using various settings can aid in students' creativity. A setting can be a portion of a classroom that can be transformed into a miniature motor lab or simply the corner of a gym. The equipment should be portable enough to be moved from one location to another.

When you have a larger population of students with severe and profound disabilities, it is easier to justify the need to secure a dedicated space. Following are several examples of spaces and equipment used for children with disabilities.

Elementary Level

- Suspended balls can be used in a classroom with ceiling panels. Use a ceiling clip and hook a chain or cord that can be adjusted to various heights for kicking and striking.
- Room dividers are ideal for stick-on items such as switch toys, mirrors, wall activity centers, and targets.
- Balance areas can contain balance boards, washtubs, and steppers.
- A sensory den is a great area for visual stimulation, suspended objects, tactile mats, tube lights, bell balls, and switch toys.

- Tunnels can include large half tunnels with suspended items.
- Minitrampolines are great for jumping and vestibular input.
- Swings can be used with support from an occupational therapist or physical therapist.
- Treadmills are a favorite among autistic students and very effective if a student can activate a movie by maintaining a steady pace. (Students should be closely monitored.)
- Rifton bikes and pony walkers are adapted bikes and walkers.
- Roller racers are self-propelled scooters.
- Jet mobiles are rolling body boards.
- Therapy balls come in all sizes.

Secondary Level

Set up a motor lab with fitness equipment to create a lifetime fitness environment:

- Treadmills are available in both manual and electric versions.
- Bike styles are recumbent, stationary, and Rifton.
- Elliptical machines are available in commercial quality or home gym versions.
- Therapy balls come in all sizes.
- Weights come in several varieties, such as barbells and medicine balls.
- Therapy bands can be long or short.

Flat Straps

NEED AND DISABILITY

This item can be used on a stand or attached to the arm of a wheelchair. Items attached to the flat straps provide visual tracking and tactile stimulation for students with severe or multiple disabilities who have limited mobility. Flat straps provide a quick way to change out items for use with multiple stands in a classroom.

TOOLS

Industrial scissors, grommet installation kit

SUPPLIES

1 1-1/2-inch flat strap (used dog leashes if possible) in multiple colors

6 to 8 snaps or grommets

INSTRUCTIONS

1. Cut straps in multiple lengths.

2. Burn ends to keep from unraveling.

3. Hammer grommets or put in snaps on each end.

4. A variety of connections gives you more options for attaching objects.

IDEAS FOR USING THIS EQUIPMENT

- Hang the straps on a stand or attach to a wheelchair arm. Attach objects to the straps according to students' needs or the classroom topics.
- Attach switches, lights, or balls.
- Play a modified baseball game by suspending a baseball with a strap and letting the students swing at it.

MODIFICATIONS

Modify the texture and length of the straps and use snaps or buttons.

Hula Hoop Mobile

▶ NEED AND DISABILITY

This tool offers visual and tactile stimulation for students with severe or multiple disabilities who have limited mobility. A variety of objects are hooked to the mobile to provide students with visual stimulation. Textured objects and shapes are examples of items that can be added to allow students to work on reaching and grasping. This is a wonderful tool to use in a section of a classroom or gym.

▶ TOOLS

Electric drill, tape measure

▶ SUPPLIES

1 hula hoop

12 2-inch notebook rings or shower curtain rings

12 items related to theme of mobile

1 heavy string or chain

1 carabiner hook (can be purchased at a hardware store)

▶ INSTRUCTIONS

1. Drill 1/4-inch holes through the hula hoop about 4 to 6 inches apart all the way around hoop.

2. Thread the string or chain through three spots spread evenly around the hula hoop.

3. Thread notebook rings through holes and attach inserted sensory objects of your choice to rings.

4. Bring ends of chain or string together and attach to the carabiner hook.

5. Hang at desired height from ceiling, stand (you can make one using PVC pipes), or basketball goal. The position will depend on whether the student is lying on a wedge mat, lying on a flat mat, or sitting. The height varies according to the sitting or lying position, so objects will hang for easy reaching or eye gazing.

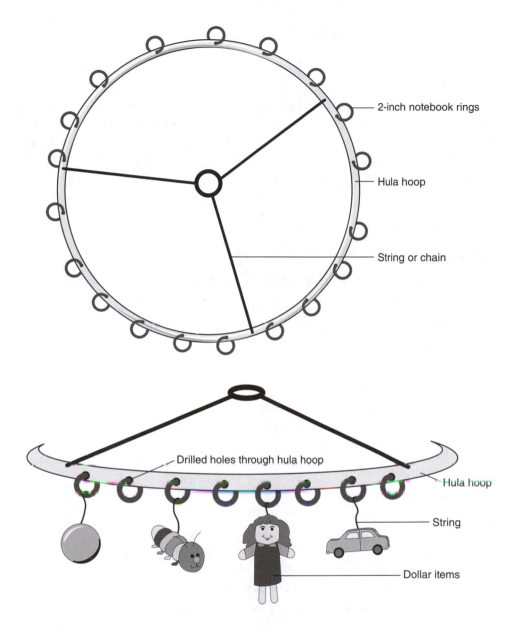

2-inch notebook rings

Hula hoop

String or chain

Drilled holes through hula hoop

Hula hoop

String

Dollar items

▶ IDEAS FOR USING THIS EQUIPMENT

You could use themes to guide the selection of objects. For example, use objects specific to a season, a reading unit, a sport, or particular self-help skills you're working on.

Under an Umbrella

▶NEED AND DISABILITY

This is more portable than the hula hoop mobile. It can be easily attached to a student's chair, desk, or wheelchair. Objects of various textures and shapes are added to allow students to work on reaching and grasping. Under an umbrella is a tool that offers visual and tactile stimulation for students with severe or multiple disabilities who have limited mobility.

▶TOOLS

None needed

▶SUPPLIES

1 small umbrella with clamp (such as one for the beach or a golf cart)

4 medium-size jingle bells

1 pompom (any color)

4 balloons

1 Slinky

1 lit cheerleading pom-pom

2 Mardi Gras-style beads

1 string of battery-operated Christmas lights

4 batteries

1 gift-wrapping ribbon

Zip ties, hair bands, or binder rings

▶INSTRUCTIONS

1. Attach items around umbrella using zip ties, hair bands, or binder rings. Make sure each item is secured.

2. Lights should be woven in and out inside the top of the umbrella.

3. Attach umbrella to a student's chair or wheelchair.

▶ IDEAS FOR USING THIS EQUIPMENT

Change items as desired to students' needs (various-size balls, objects, textures, beads, kitchen items, colors, weather items, shiny items). You could use themes to guide the selection of objects. For example, use objects specific to a season, a reading unit, a sport, or particular self-help skills you're working on.

▶ MODIFICATIONS

- Use large umbrella with umbrella stand for multiple students to use.
- Use more lights and more objects at different heights.

Portable A-Frame Stand

▶ NEED AND DISABILITY

This tool has multiple uses. The hanging items offer students with severe and multiple disabilities the ability to push, kick, grasp, and pull objects. The varied heights provide students in wheelchairs with multilevel and multisensory experiences. This tool offers visual and tactile stimulation for students who have limited mobility. The portable A-frame stand can be set up wherever the physical education class may be, and it folds easily, which makes for a quick setup.

▶ TOOLS

Hand saw or electric saw, electric drill (1/4-inch bit), tape measure

▶ SUPPLIES

- 3 1-inch PVC piping 10 feet long
- 2 1-inch elbow joints
- 2 1-inch end caps
- 2 1-inch T-joints
- 4 rubber stoppers
- 2 3-inch wing nut bolts
- 4 small hanging hooks
- 2 16-inch pieces of chain or cord
- 1 container of PVC glue

▶ INSTRUCTIONS

1. Cut PVC into two 1-foot lengths, two 3-foot lengths, two 4-foot lengths, and two 5-foot lengths.
2. Using one 3-foot section of PVC, attach the two 5-foot sections with two elbow joints.
3. Using one 4-foot section, attach one of the T-joints with 1-foot section together. Repeat with other 4-foot section and 1-foot section.

4. Using a 3-foot section, attach to the remaining joints of the T-joint as in the diagram.

5. While lying on floor, line up the two sections and drill hole through both pieces approximately 12 inches from the top.

6. Take the 3-1/2-inch bolt and push through both pieces; secure both sections together.

7. Each of the sections should be able to move back and forth for height adjustments or storage.

8. Push rubber stoppers onto ends of PVC that are in contact with floor.

9. For stability, twist hooks into PVC about 12 inches from bottom and hook chain to both hooks, as shown in the diagram. Glue for stability.

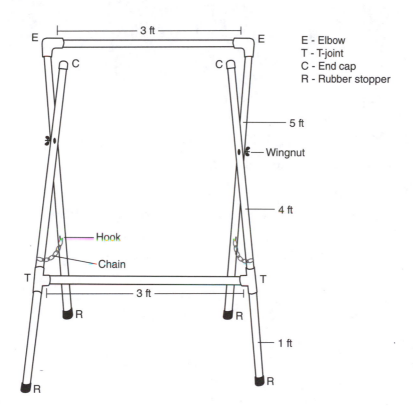

E - Elbow
T - T-joint
C - End cap
R - Rubber stopper

(continued)

Portable A-Frame Stand   *(continued)*

▶IDEAS FOR USING THIS EQUIPMENT

Use as a mobile or suspend balls to be hit or kicked.

▶MODIFICATIONS

- Different heights and widths can be cut to accommodate various sizes of wheelchairs.
- Use colored tape to make it more visible.

Modified Wristband

▶ NEED AND DISABILITY

These tools provide students with visual, auditory, and tactile stimulation literally in the palms of their hands. Students with emerging skills will work on crossing the midline and manipulative skills without leaving their chairs or mats. Portable, lightweight, and easily stored, the modified wristbands are essential for any motor lab environment.

▶ TOOLS

Scissors, tape measure, thread, needle

▶ SUPPLIES

1 wristband in a variety of colors

6 to 8 bells (the kind with a hook on the bell)

▶ INSTRUCTIONS

Sew bells to wristband, equally spaced atop the wrist on one side of band.

▶ IDEAS FOR USING THIS EQUIPMENT

- Play tag. The person who is It wears the bells.
- The band can also be worn on the feet, providing sensory stimulation.

▶ MODIFICATIONS

- Attach bells to cuffs of long-sleeve T-shirt.
- Wristbands with bells can also be used for modifying jump rope lead-up skills. When jumping rope, slip handle through wristband so the student will not let go of the rope. It can also be used for auditory stimulation. The wristbands can also hold items for other activities, such as balloon toss: The balloon is attached to a string and a wristband (but the student isn't wearing the band on the wrist). That way, the student can easily retrieve the balloon by grabbing the wristband.
- Bells on bands can be slipped over shoes for gait training.

Sensory Room

NEED AND DISABILITY

The sensory room allows students with severe or multiple disabilities who have limited mobility to gain visual and tactile stimulation through tracking and motor planning. The size of the room varies according to allowances for space and students' needs. Hanging objects allow for reaching and grasping. The lights attached to the top or sides give students visual stimulation. A student can lie or sit in a sensory room with limited distractions and create a world of their own.

TOOLS

Hand saw or PVC pipe cutter, tape measure

SUPPLIES

   2-inch PVC pipe 35 feet long

   8 2-inch T-joints

   4 2-inch 90-degree elbow joints

   8 2-inch end caps

   1 container of PVC glue

INSTRUCTIONS

1. Cut PVC into two 3-foot lengths, six 4-foot lengths, four 3-inch lengths, and eight 6-inch lengths.
2. Make all cuts and assemble according to the diagram.
3. Gluing is an option for assembly.
4. Depending on your storage needs, you might want to glue certain joints for easier assembly.

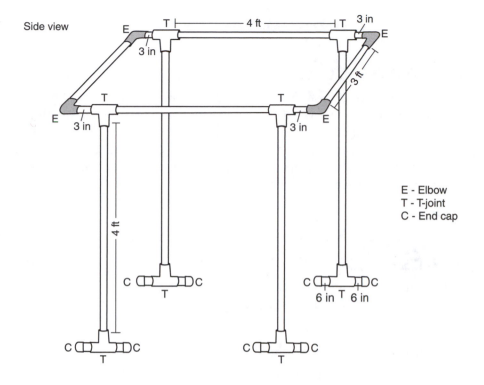

Side view

E - Elbow
T - T-joint
C - End cap

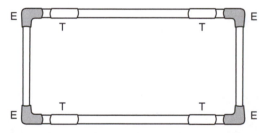

Top view

▶ IDEAS FOR USING THIS EQUIPMENT

The room is usually used for students with severe sensory problems. It offers sensory input without distractions. It provides sensory stimulation rather than a specific activity.

▶ MODIFICATIONS

- Place a small parachute over top and sides. In the den you can hang a ball, scarves, a shiny object or objects, and mini-pinwheels.
- Place clear plastic Plexiglass over the top with holes in it and put lights around the top. Hang items from the top.
- Also use the same frame with shorter legs to make a dry-erase tabletop.

Ambulatory Trainer

▶NEED AND DISABILITY

This tool is used for non-ambulatory students with emerging walking skills. The ambulatory trainer was developed for gait training in a safe walking program. A walking program encourages development of gross motor skills, which go hand in hand with weight bearing and promote functional and cognitive improvements. The ambulatory trainer should be used only under the direct supervision of a physical therapist.

▶TOOLS

Hand saw or electric saw, electric drill (1/2-inch bit), tape measure

▶SUPPLIES

4 2-inch PVC pipes 10 feet long

1 2-1/2-inch PVC pipe 12 feet long

6 3-1/4-inch bolts with nuts

1 piece of lightweight plywood 4 by 8 feet

4 2-inch PVC 90-degree elbow joints

2 2-inch T-joints

6 2-1/2-inch PVC couplings

24 screws

▶INSTRUCTIONS

1. Cut 2-inch PVC into four 4-foot lengths and six 3-foot lengths.

2. Cut 2-1/2-inch PVC into six 2-foot lengths.

3. Drill into the 2-inch PVC three or four 1/4-inch holes at one end of each section.

4. Drill into the 2-1/2-inch PVC one 1/4-inch hole in the top of each section.

5. Assemble as shown in the diagram.

6. An option is to cut hand holes in bottom of plywood for easy travel.

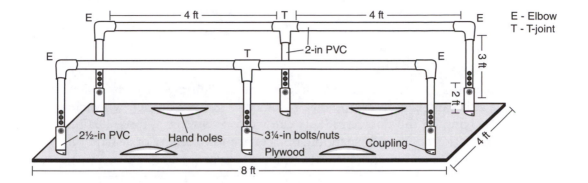

▶IDEAS FOR USING THIS EQUIPMENT

- Swing on bars to improve muscular strength.
- Jump over or leap over area on plank.
- Walk on tiptoes to improve muscular strength in legs.

▶MODIFICATION

Once a student has acquired some balance, increase the difficulty by taking one side off.

Therapy Bed

▶ NEED AND DISABILITY

The cost of a therapy bed can be exorbitant. Building your own is simple. Using a therapy bed gives students a chance to get out of their wheelchairs without lying on the floor. Students can work on strength, tone, flexibility, and isometric activities. Suspending objects from the ceiling or a stand offers additional stimulation and options for more activities.

▶ TOOLS

Hand saw or electric saw, hammer, square, tape measure, sawhorse

▶ SUPPLIES

1 sheet of plywood 4 feet by 8 feet by 1/2 inch

7 boards 2 inches by 4 inches by 8 feet

1 4-by-4-inch cedar post 9 feet long

6 trim boards 1 inch by 2 inches by 8 feet

1 folding mat 4 by 8 feet

1 box heavy nails

▶ INSTRUCTIONS

1. Set two of the 2-inch-by-4-inch-by-8-foot boards aside while cutting the other five boards. These two will be used to construct the therapy bed.

2. Using a sawhorse, cut five of the 2-inch-by-4-inch-by-8-foot boards into five 2-by-4-by-44-inch lengths and eight support pieces. Lengths of support pieces will vary depending on distance between 44-inch support beams.

3. Sizes will vary depending on placements.

4. After form is constructed as in the diagram, cut the 4-by-4-inch post into four pieces, each 18 inches long. Attach to four corners using heavy-duty nails, nailing from outside edges.

5. Six posts can be used for better stability as shown in the diagram.

6. Turn over to continue instructions.

7. Nail 4-by-8-foot plywood on top. Make sure it is flush with edges.

8. Using trim wood, attach from post to post around the whole bed to give extra support. This can be added approximately half the distance from the floor.

9. Add mat for comfort.

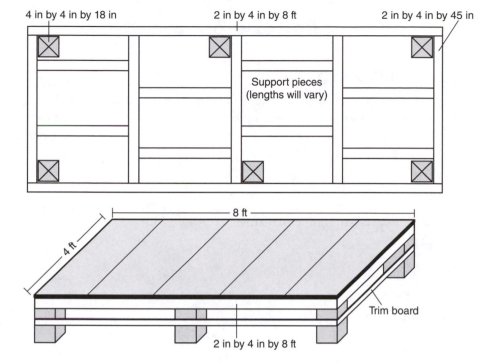

4 in by 4 in by 18 in   2 in by 4 in by 8 ft   2 in by 4 in by 45 in

Support pieces
(lengths will vary)

8 ft

4 ft

Trim board

2 in by 4 in by 8 ft

▶ IDEAS FOR USING THIS EQUIPMENT

While student is on the therapy bed, you can do the following:

- Place a tunnel with hanging objects over student.
- Suspend balls from ceiling so the student can kick or hit them with hands or head.
- Place mobile over student to provide stimulus.

▶ MODIFICATIONS

Make legs of the bed higher to accommodate wheelchair height. Students lying on the mat should always be closely supervised.

Tactile Mat

▶ NEED AND DISABILITY

This is a tool that offers visual and tactile stimulation for students with severe and multiple disabilities. Using the tactile mat allows students to feel a variety of textures using upper-body strength while moving around the tactile mat. Students will gain sensory stimulation, work on crossing the midline, and strengthen muscles.

▶ TOOLS

Sewing machine, scissors, tape measure

▶ SUPPLIES

Old plain quilt

AstroTurf scraps

Door mats (scratchy type)

Various carpet pieces, such as shag, Berber, plush

Any fun tactile items from a dollar store

▶ INSTRUCTIONS

1. Sew a variety of textures, materials, and scraps to the quilt. This is a touchy-feely mat for students.
2. Attach a variety of items to the mat.
3. The mat can be placed on the floor in a sensory motor lab.

▶ IDEAS FOR USING THIS EQUIPMENT

Allow students to explore and crawl on mat. Play Twister.

▶ MODIFICATIONS

Mat can be made of tablecloths, placemats (for a smaller version), or with Velcro sections so it can be changed.

Rainmaker and Sensory Bottle

▶NEED AND DISABILITY

Rainmakers and sensory bottles offer visual, auditory, and tactile stimulation for students with severe or multiple intellectual disabilities. Students with emerging developmental skills have the opportunity to work on crossing the midline, visual tracking, focusing, and manipulative skills. This is a great item to use in a miniature motor lab, which offers hands-on enjoyment.

▶TOOLS

Scissors

▶SUPPLIES

Various-size water bottles, 12 to 24 ounces in a variety of shapes

Glitter

Food coloring

Strands of beads cut in 2-inch strips

Colored pipe cleaners in 1- to 2-inch strips

Sequins

Any item that looks cool in a bottle

Colorful aquarium stones

Vegetable oil

Glue

▶INSTRUCTIONS

1. Remove labels from bottles.
2. Put pipe cleaners and a teaspoon of glitter, sequins, or beads in bottle.
3. Fill bottle with water and place one or two drops of food coloring and a teaspoon of oil in bottle.
4. Glue lid on and cover lid with colored electrical tape.
5. You have an instant sensory water bottle. Shake it and watch the items move. To make a rainmaker, do not add water; instead, add small colorful aquarium stones. Glue lid and secure with tape.

▶IDEAS FOR USING THIS EQUIPMENT

Use as a shaker for spirit events, noisemaker, timer, and buzzer for games.

▶MODIFICATIONS

Use different-size bottles using noisy objects instead of oil.

Sensory Box

NEED AND DISABILITY

This tool offers visual and tactile stimulation for students with severe or multiple intellectual disabilities. Students with emerging skills can work on crossing the midline, manipulative skills, reaching, and grasping.

TOOLS

Scissors, tape measure

SUPPLIES

1 shoe box (any size)

1 package of wrapping paper (any color or style)

Strings of beads of various styles

1 roll of tape or bottle of glue

INSTRUCTIONS

1. Line the inside of the shoe box with wrapping paper.
2. Punch a small hole on the side of the shoe box to push the beads through.
3. Tie off or tape beads on the outside of the box.
4. Cut the length of the bead strings to the width of the box so they hang without touching the bottom when the box is on its side.
5. Wrap the outside of the box to hide tape.

IDEAS FOR USING THIS EQUIPMENT

Students can run fingers through beads, reaching and grasping. Higher-level students can make it a counting activity.

MODIFICATIONS

- Put sandpaper on the bottom of the box, or hang streamers instead of beads.
- Use any table, box, or chair to attach beads to.

Sensory Balls

NEED AND DISABILITY

These tools offer visual and tactile stimulation for students with severe or multiple intellectual disabilities. Students have a variety of balls to squeeze and manipulate with their hands. These homemade balls provide stress relief and a remedy for fidgeting.

TOOLS

Scissors

SUPPLIES

Surplus pantyhose

Dry beans

Rice

Latex-free balloons

Funnel

INSTRUCTIONS

1. Cut off the top of the pantyhose. Cut the legs into 6-inch strips and tie a knot on one end of each.
2. Turn it inside out so the knot is on the inside.
3. Using a funnel, place 1 cup of beans or rice into the hose, then tie another knot to make a ball.
4. Cut off the end of a balloon and work it over the ball.
5. Use another balloon to secure the opening so that the ball is covered with two balloons.

IDEAS FOR USING THIS EQUIPMENT

Sensory balls can be used in a beanbag toss or in catch and release exercises.

MODIFICATIONS

Use other materials inside the hose (such as sand or flour).

Sensory Lap Tray

NEED AND DISABILITY

This is a tool for students with severe intellectual disabilities. The sensory lap tray is great for students with limited mobility; it encourages sensory processing, motor planning, auditory and tactile stimulation, and visual skill. Students with emerging skills have the opportunity to work on reaching and grasping.

TOOLS

Electric drill (1/4-inch bit), tape measure, hammer, hand or electric saw

SUPPLIES

1 piece of peg board 2 by 2 feet

1 trim board 1 inch by 1 inch by 10 feet

Box of 1/2-inch nails

1 bottle of wood glue

6 to 8 zip ties

6 to 8 sensory objects (bells, squeeze toys, plush animals, brushes, sponges)

INSTRUCTIONS

1. Cut trim board into two 2-foot lengths and two 22-inch lengths.
2. On back of peg board, attach trim board around edges for stability with 1/2-inch nails or wood glue.
3. Reinforce the seal by using wood glue as you attach the trim boards.
4. Turn peg board over and slip zip ties down and back up the predrilled holes in board.
5. Attach objects as desired.

IDEAS FOR USING THIS EQUIPMENT

This can be used as a laptop surface on wheelchairs or tables. Transfer it to the floor or use it in a sensory light box for additional stimulation.

MODIFICATIONS

- Change the objects for various thematic units.
- Use old discarded wheelchair trays, food trays, and high chair trays.

Sensory Lap Towel

▶ NEED AND DISABILITY

This is a good tool for students with severe intellectual disabilities. A sensory lap towel encourages cognitive activity, sensory processing, motor planning, auditory and tactile stimulation, and visual skills. Students with emerging skills have the opportunity to work on reaching and grasping.

▶ TOOLS

Sewing machine with thread, scissors, tape measure

▶ SUPPLIES

1 hand towel or scarf

1/2-inch-wide elastic band 16 inches long

2 sections of Velcro 12 to 16 inches long

▶ INSTRUCTIONS

1. Sew Velcro strips so they go down the towel in two parallel lines 5 inches apart.
2. Sew one end of the elastic band on one side of the top of towel 2 inches from the edge. Repeat with the other end of the elastic band on the other side of the top of towel. This will make a strap to put around the student's neck.
3. Attach the Velcro to any object as shown in the diagram.

▶ IDEAS FOR USING THIS EQUIPMENT

This is used as a laptop surface on wheelchairs or tables. Transfer it to the floor or use it in a sensory light box for additional stimulation.

▶ MODIFICATIONS

Rather than a hand towel or scarf, you can use a placemat or tablecloth. Objects can be changed based on thematic units.

Appendix

Everyday Items Transformed

Tight budgets and exorbitant costs of purchased equipment call for ways to transform junk into jewels and trash into treasures. This appendix presents items designed and used for one thing but are now transformed into something entirely different.

Most are common items that can be transformed into physical education equipment or assistive devices for learning. Some of these devices will serve as tools to reinforce previously taught skills. All students, whether they participate in the general physical education setting or in adapted physical education classes, can use the items.

HOUSEHOLD ITEMS

Items generally found around the home can be transformed into equipment for the physical education setting at minimal cost.

Items	Purpose or use
Pipe insulation	Racket handles perfect for students with gripping problems
Swim noodles	Bowling pins cut in 8-inch lengths
	Tag games
	Jump ropes
	Game tokens (these make great discs and pucks)
Plastic trash bags	Juggling
Salad servers	Grasping object from wheelchair
Pantyhose	Stretch bands
	Beanbags
	Sensory balls
	Deck rings
	Toss rings
Laundry bags	Equipment bags
	Potato sack races
Spring-loaded mesh hampers	Basketball targets

(continued)

121

Household Items *(continued)*

Items	Purpose or use
Storage tubs	Target tubs Baskets
Kitchen sink tubs	Target tubs Sensory stimulation tubs
Flat bed sheets	Hanging targets
Shower curtains	Hanging targets

RECYCLED PRODUCTS

Recycled items are generally found around the home. Giving parents a suggestion list will bring you an ample supply of items to be transformed.

Items	Purpose or use
Pringles cans	Tape ribbon to inside of lid, squeeze
Plastic soft drink bottles	Tees for bigger balls (cut off bottom of bottle, turn upside down, and place the ball in the tee)
Milk bottles	Ball toss scoops Scoops Weights (fill with sand, rocks, or water and seal)
Cream bottles	Bowling pins Shakers (bells)
Mint containers	Hockey pucks
Plastic lids	Frisbees Game pieces or pucks
Water bottles	Directional sound objects when filled with rocks Sensory bottles
Coffee containers	Drums
Shoe boxes	Sensory boxes, skates, skis
Cardboard tubes (all sorts)	Striking equipment
Tennis ball cans	Color or object sorting Object for manipulative development Shakers Visual trackers "I Spy" (fill can with filler such as rice or beans and put objects in it to find)

LOST AND FOUND

Discarded items are found around the home, neighborhood, and construction sites. Discarded items are generally free; with minimal cost, they are transformed into useful equipment. The following items can be used in all physical education programs.

Items	Purpose or use
Dog leash	Straps for suspending items
Lampshade	Funnels, catching things
Lumber	Building things as needed
Discarded pipe	Stands for sensory room, mobiles
School chairs	Scooter boards
Nuts, bolts, and screws	Sorting, fine motor activities Counting
Jump ropes	Guide ropes Pulley for scooter boards
Basketball cut in half	Balance and stepping stones

ITEMS FOR SENSORY STIMULATION

The following items are found everywhere. Most students with severe intellectual disabilities have tactile system imbalance (they are sensitive to touch). Any of the items are ideal for exploration activities if placed in a tub or baby pool. Students have fun scooping, pouring, and sorting the items, which help with fine motor skills. *To prevent choking or ingestion, closely supervise all students using any of these items.*

Items	Purpose or use
Water	Floating items, boats, fish, bubbles
Sand	Use wet for molding; bury items to find
Dry macaroni	Can be colored and strung; sort by colors and shapes
Leaves	Put leaves in tub and have students crush and feel difference between dry and green leaves
Acorns, nuts	Sort, count, and touch; make ornaments

(continued)

Items for Sensory Stimulation   *(continued)*

Items	Purpose or use
Pine cones	Sort, count, and touch; make ornaments
Shredded paper	Use colored paper to hide small items in tub to find
Popcorn	Use to scoop and touch; make ornaments
Dried corn	Feel dried corn on the cob; use loose corn to scoop and touch
Plastic snow	Use to scoop and touch
Rice	Use to scoop and touch
Shaving cream	Touch, draw letters in it
Puff balls	Use to scoop and feel
Wood chips	Use cedar to smell, scoop, and feel
Easter grass	Add eggs for Easter egg hunts; use for stuffing in containers; build nests
Dirt or mud	Bury bones and treasures and go on a dig; add water and make mud and form designs
Paper confetti	Fill plastic eggs for fiesta
Foil confetti	Add coins and hunt for treasures
Paperclips	Sort, scoop, use magnets
Packing peanuts	Use to scoop, put in containers
Rocks	Use to scoop, sort, and touch
Coffee grounds	Use to scoop, touch, and smell
	Use as pretend dirt with little trucks and cars
Birdseed	Use to scoop and touch; use in bird feeders
Nuts and bolts	Great for sorting; fit the nuts and bolts together
Sawdust	Use to scoop; feel texture
Rock salt	Use to scoop and touch
Jell-O	Watch jiggling effect; feel texture; cube and eat
Pudding or tapioca	Observe texture, taste
Cooked pasta	Use forks and spoons for twirling
Bubble wrap	Squeeze and pop, stomp and pop

Glossary

AstroTurf—Brand of artificial turf. Although the term is a registered trademark, it is sometimes used as a generic description of any kind of artificial turf.

balance disc—Inflated rubber cushion with low nubs on one side and raised nubs on the other.

big mac—Button or switch that uses digital technology to allow simple sound recording for up to 20 seconds. It has an on/off switch, volume control, and one-shot timer to prevent sound repetition.

brad—Also known as a split pin or brass fastener. A soft-metal item used for securing multiple sheets of paper together. The fastener is inserted into punched holes in the stack of paper. The leaves, or tines, of the legs are of unequal lengths; they are separated and bent over to secure the paper. This holds the pin in place and the sheets of paper together. Commonly used in situations that require rotation around a joint, such as mobile paper and cardboard models. Shaped somewhat like a nail with a round head and flat, split length. Similar in design and function to the mechanical counterpart cotter pins.

carabiner—Steel or aluminum loop with a sprung or screwed gate that is used to quickly and reversibly connect components. Widely used in rope-intensive activities such as climbing, caving, sailing, construction, and window cleaning. Carabiners used in sports tend to be of a lighter weight than those used in industrial rope work and rope rescue.

carabiner hook—Sprung swinging gate that accepts a rope, webbing sling, or other hardware. Rock climbers frequently connect two nonlocking carabiners with a short length of nylon web to create a quick draw.

card stock—Paper stock stiff enough for the printing of business cards and similar uses.

caster—Small wheel on a swivel, set under a piece of furniture or a machine, to facilitate moving it.

circular saw—Metal disc or blade with saw teeth on the edge; also the machine that causes the disc to spin. A tool for cutting wood or other materials; may be handheld or table mounted. Can also be used to make narrow slots (dados). Most of these saws cut wood but may also be equipped with a blade that cuts masonry, plastic, or metal. Some circular saws are specially designed for particular materials.

compass—Instrument used for drawing circles and measuring distances; consists of two arms, joined at one end. One arm serves as a pivot point, while the other is extended or describes a circle.

deck ring—Also referred to as pool deck ring. Made of easy-to-grasp soft rubber; can also be made from the legs of pantyhose. Spongy rubber rings are brightly colored and sturdy. They will not scratch or mark floors, so they're perfect for indoors or out. Used for various catching and tossing activities.

dowel—Solid cylindrical rod usually made of wood, plastic, or metal. In its original manufactured form, dowel is called *dowel rod*.

drill bit—Cutting tools used to create round holes. Bits are held in a tool called a drill, which rotates them and provides torque and axial force to create the hole. Specialized bits are also available for noncylindrical-shaped holes. The shank is the part of the drill bit grasped by the chuck of a drill. The cutting edges of the drill bit are at one end, and the shank is at the other. Drill bits come in various sizes.

electrical tape—Type of pressure-sensitive tape used to insulate electrical wires and other materials that conduct electricity. Can be made of many plastics, but vinyl is most popular because it stretches well and gives long-lasting insulation. Electrical tape for class H insulation is made of fiberglass cloth.

foam board—Resilient polystyrene foam core board found in craft stores.

gripper drawer liner—Nonstick soft rubber matting used for lining a drawer.

grommet—Ring of metal, plastic, or rubber that reinforced a hole or protects sharp edges of a hole. Widely used in clothing, industrial, and surgical applications. Also referred to as eyelets. Usually made of metal and composed of two parts, front and back, that encase the edges of the hole.

grommet installation kit—Contains a supply of grommets along with the tools for completing a grommet project in a few simple steps. Available in several sizes; additional parts are sold separately.

gym tape—Used for marking gym floors.

hand saw—Any common saw with a handle at one end for manual operation with one hand used for cutting wood.

hole cutter—Saw consisting of a metal cylinder, usually steel, mounted on an arbor. The cutting edge either has saw teeth formed in it or industrial diamonds embedded in it. The arbor can carry a drill bit to bore a centering hole. After the first few millimeters are cut, the centering mechanism may no longer be needed, although it will help the bit to bore without wandering in a deep hole. The sloping slots in the cylinder wall help carry dust out. The width of the cut is designed to be slightly larger than the diameter of the rest of the hole saw so that it does not get jammed in the hole.

juggling scarve—17-square-inch nylon fabric.

masking tape—Easily removed adhesive tape used temporarily for defining margins and protecting surfaces, as when painting. Sometimes used for binding, sealing, or mending.

MDF board—Medium-density fiberboard (MDF). Engineered product formed by breaking down hardwood or softwood residuals into wood fibers, combining it with wax and a resin binder, and forming panels by applying high temperature and pressure. MDF is denser than plywood.

milk crate—Square or rectangular interlocking boxes that are used to transport milk and other products from dairies to retail establishments. Also referred to as storage crates.

notebook rings—Metal or plastic rings used to secure paper to a notebook.

painter's tape—Type of masking tape usually used for wall painting.

paneling—Interior wall covering used as an alternative to the more common textured or painted drywall and wallpaper.

pipe insulation—Thermal or acoustic insulation used on pipe work. Used to prevent heat loss and gain from pipes and to save energy.

plywood—Material used for various building purposes. Consists of an odd number of veneers glued over each other, usually at right angles.

PVC cutter—Tool used for cutting PVC pipe. Handle is ergonomically designed and is grooved so that the blade can be pivoted and locked into multiple positions.

PVC glue—Type of cement that is used for PVC pipe. Can fill holes and cracks in PVC pipe, securely connect new PVC pipe, and keep loose pipes together. Also known as PVC solvent cement.

PVC pipe—Abbreviated term for polyvinyl chloride, a plastic compound that is flexible, lightweight, and easy to use.

round molding—Raw wood ready for finishing. Acts as a retainer for wood or glass panels.

rubber stopper—Sometimes called a rubber bung. Truncated cylindrical or conical closure to seal a container, such as a bottle, tube, or barrel. Unlike a lid, which encloses a container from the outside without displacing the inner volume, a rubber stopper is partially inserted inside the container to act as a seal. Also used on the bottom of canes and walkers.

seat cushion—Soft bag of cloth, leather, or rubber filled with feathers, air, or foam rubber. Used as padding for sitting, kneeling, or lying down.

Softi ball—Ball made of foam, sponge, rubber, or yarn.

speed jump rope—Jump rope that combines speed with weight; used for developing aerobic power and stamina. Adjustable 10-foot-long durable solid rubber rope with molded handles, foam grips, and sealed ball bearings for even rotation.

Styrofoam ball—Polystyrene foam in a spherical shape. Often used for craft applications.

swim noodle—Cylindrical piece of polyethylene foam; sometimes hollow.

token—Object, usually plastic and round, representing placement in a game.

washer—Flat ring or perforated piece of leather, rubber, or metal. Used to give tightness to a joint, prevent leakage, or distribute pressure, as under the head of a nut or bolt.

Wiffle ball—Hollow plastic ball with cutouts.

wooden ball—Carved from real wood.

zip ties—Also known as a tie wrap. Type of fastener consisting of a sturdy nylon tape with an integrated gear rack. On one end is a ratchet in a small open case.

About the Authors

(L to R) Cindy Slagle, Teresa Sullivan, Vic Brevard, T.J. Hapshie, and Debbie Brevard.

Teresa Sullivan has been teaching students with various disabilities in adapted physical education since 2002 in the North East Independent School District (NEISD) in Texas. She has been an active member of the **Texas Association for Health, Physical Education, Recreation and Dance (TAHPERD)** since 1998. Teresa has transformed the NEISD Special Olympics program into an exemplary sports program for young adults with special needs. She participates as an Area 20 Special Olympics co-head trainer and is involved in the Area Sports Management Team (ASMT) committee for the San Antonio area. In addition, she has been involved in a state-level games committee for Special Olympics Texas. Many of Teresa's athletes have competed in area, state, and international Special Olympic events. Teresa is well known for her innovation in building equipment. She has presented various workshops addressing how to build equipment for people with special needs. Teresa was awarded the Superintendent's Award for NEISD during 2005-2006 and has been named Coach of the Year and Trainer of the Year for Special Olympics Texas in Area 20.

Cindy Slagle has been an active member of the **Texas Association for Health, Physical Education, Recreation and Dance (TAHPERD)** since 1992. She has over 30 years of experience teaching adapted physical education and 16 years of service to North East Independent School District (NEISD). Cindy is responsible for leading a team of 14 adapted physical education specialists dedicated to providing testing, development, and placement to children with diverse special needs in 64 schools throughout the district. Cindy was the 2006 recipient of the Texas TAHPERD Adapted Physical Educator of the Year award and the recipient of the 2006-07 Superintendent's Award for NEISD. In February 2007 she received the Adapted Physical Education Teacher of the Year Award from the Southern District American Alliance for Health, Physical Education, Recreation and Dance. She is a graduate of Kansas State University. Cindy has presented numerous district in-service workshops and has been a presenter at more than 30 state and national conferences, most notably the National Conference on Physical Activity for the Exceptional Individual, New York State AHPERD, the National AAHPERD Conference, and the Midwest Symposium of Therapeutic Recreation and Physical Activities. Cindy receives great satisfaction sharing her experiences with her colleagues while expanding her knowledge base.

Thelma (TJ) Hapshie, is a certified adapted physical educator with more than 40 years of experience working with people with developmental, physical, and emotional disabilities. She has worked at the San Antonio State Hospital and the San Antonio State School, private and public schools, recreation centers, and group homes. TJ has been an active member of TAHPERD for 14 years. She is a graduate of Incarnate Word College. She has invented and patented a device that provides auditory cues to assist individuals with visual impairments in bowling independently.

TJ has presented at numerous district in-service workshops, several state national conferences (most notably the National Conference on Physical Activity for the Exceptional Individual, TAHPERD, New York State AHPERD, and the National AAHPERD Conference). She was named Adapted Physical Educator of the Year by TAHPERD in 2009, the Recreation Professional of the Year by TAHPERD in 2011, and the Recreation Professional of the Year by the Southern District American Alliance for Health, Physical Education, Recreation and Dance in 2011-2012.

Vic Brevard has been an educator since 1989. He coached football, basketball, track, and tennis for 8 years (4 years with Refugio Independent School District and 4 years in Ft. Bend Independent School District in Texas). He was the middle school sport coordinator at both school districts and was and the team leader for the Alief ISD adapted physical education program. Vic is the recipient of the 2008 Texas TAHPERD Adapted Physical Educator of the Year Award.

Debbie Brevard taught for 28 years. She started out in Andrews at the high school, where she was the cheerleader coach. After moving to Refugio, she coached high school volleyball, middle school basketball, and track. Debbie was the head track coach and assistant volleyball coach at Kempner High School in Ft. Bend, Texas. She then worked as an elementary physical education teacher. She taught adapted physical education for five years.